PITIFUL or POWERFUL

THE CHOICE IS YOURS

PITIFUL or POWERFUL

THE CHOICE IS YOURS

by Dr. Rachel V. Jeffries

BOLD TRUTH
PUBLISHING

Christian Literature & Artwork

A BOLD TRUTH Publication

PURPOSE OF THIS BOOK

PITIFUL OR POWERFUL - THE CHOICE IS YOURS

The purpose of this book and workbook combination is to help you become more powerful instead of pitiful. God wants us to be healed SPIRIT, SOUL AND BODY. We are created for a purpose and God wants us to fulfill that purpose. When we walk in our purpose, we walk in God's highest call for our lives.

This book and workbook is designed to help you receive healing in the area of your emotions. There are hindrances that keep us blinded to our purpose. We are going to deal with many of these issues. You will be able to examine yourself with the help of the Holy Spirit, get over self-pity, and have power in your life. We cannot be pitiful and powerful at the same time.

If you were unaware that God has a purpose for your life, this workbook will help you find that purpose and help you start moving your life toward fulfilling that purpose.

This book deals with six sections. Each section will cover various topics within that particular subject.

Some people have no idea that God has a wonderful plan for their life. We are each here on this earth for a specific purpose and reason.

If you were the result of an unwanted pregnancy, divorced, suffering from physical illness, serious loss, have a past that seems to haunt your present, or feel rejected, God has a plan and a purpose for you.

> *Jeremiah 29:11 AMP*
> *For I know the thoughts and plans that I have for you, says the Lord, thoughts and plans for welfare and not for evil to give you hope in your final outcome.*

The definition of *thoughts* in this Scripture is intention and purpose. The meaning of the word *welfare* is completeness, safety, health, prosperity, and contentment.

We can paraphrase *Jeremiah 29:11* to read: *I the Lord know the intention and the purpose that I have for you. I have intentions and purposes to give you completeness, safety, health, prosperity, and contentment in your life.*

There are root issues that hinder us from walking in His purpose.

These roots are in our soul area. We can be born again in our spirit and still have problems that have to be dealt with in the soul. There are lots of church people who have never allowed Jesus to be Lord over their mind, will and emotions. I pray that before you finish this workbook you will be healed and able to help others to be healed.

Let us become mature and eat of the Word of God and not remain on milk only. [*Galatians 4:14 AMP*]

Hebrews 5:12 Meat is Truth

Are you prepared for what God has for you? Blessings of opportunity, relationships, favor, being in the right place at the right time, finances, and healing; these are what God has for us and it gives Him great pleasure to see us accept and receive them.

PITIFUL or POWERFUL

ISBN 10: 0-9972586-9-1
ISBN 13: 978-0-9972586-9-1

Rachel Jeffries International Ministries
P.O. Box 815
Hollister, MO 65673
www.rjim.org
racheljeffries@msn.com

BOLD TRUTH PUBLISHING *(Christian Literature & Artwork)*
606 West 41st, Ste. 4
Sand Springs, Oklahoma 74067
www.BoldTruthPublishing.com
boldtruthbooks@yahoo.com

Printed in the USA.
10 9 8 7 6 5 4 3 2 1

PERMISSIONS

PERMISSIONS

CONTENTS

CONTENTS

PREFACE

Spiritual Immaturity

Hebrews 5:12 NKJV
For though by this time you ought to be teachers, you need someone to teach you again the first principles of the oracles of God; and you have come to need milk and not solid food.

Don't give your future to your past. Don't look back. Let go of regret. Love, forgive.

"You can hurt yourself more by trying to keep yourself from being hurt."
-- Francine Rivers

"I have gone through some terrible things in my life, some of what actually happened."
-- Mark Twain

Get rid of 'I should' and 'ought to.' Should and ought to make unenforceable expectations for others and ourselves.

Instead 'I choose to,' as *Deuteronomy 30:19* says,

"I call heaven and earth as witnesses today against you, that I have set before you life and death, blessing and cursing; therefore choose life, that both you and your descendants may live;"

As you study this book, I believe you will make great choices for your life and be restored in every area that needs restoration.

AUTHOR'S NOTE

This writing was birthed out of my spirit. In 1998 a tragedy came to my life that for some would have ended their hope of any kind of profitable future. I was living in a state of feeling helpless. I needed direction and hope. When the tragedy materialized, I happened to be praying in tongues for many hours. God lifted me above the situation and kept me sane and functioning. I had a choice to make, to either be pitiful or powerful. My spirit man knew the two could not live in the same house *(spiritual house)*.

James 3:11 AMP
Does a fountain send forth [simultaneously] from the same opening fresh water and bitter?

All of my circumstances when looked at in the natural would make you pitiful looking. Inside I knew I could not allow that. I could talk pitiful or I could talk powerful. Was I hurt? Of course my emotions were very pained.

I had many questions concerning why this or that. What had I done wrong? If I had tried one more thing perhaps this would not have happened. I searched my heart. I had to come to the realization that blame is one of the symptoms of grieving.

This is where we can get into real trouble. Blaming is one of the first symptoms that tries to appear after a tragedy. This is where families often times get into strife with each other due to blaming each other. If you had only done thus and so or if I had done this or that it would not have happened. In the first heading of this book, **DEALING WITH GRIEF**, we will cover this symptom of grieving.

I am here to tell you I lived and came forth into a new freedom I had never had previously. This book is a living testimony of how good and wonderful our God is.

I share my heart with you and know exactly what you are sensing. You do have a choice to either wallow in self-pity or to decide you are going to make something great out of this with the help of the Holy Spirit. That latter choice is what makes you a powerful person instead of a pitiful person.

I encourage you to dive into this book and not set it aside. Denial will paralyze you and keep you from functioning properly. My prayer is for you to be made free and have a great life no matter what happened to you previously. You are being covered with prayer as I write this today.

"Open their eyes Lord to see who they are in Christ and just how good things are for them in the present and future. Amen."

ARE YOU PITIFUL OR POWERFUL?

We are going to start with some of the root causes as to why some people never get into their purpose in life. These things have to do with our soul area. We can be born again in our spirit and still have problems that have to be dealt with in the soul area. Some of the things we will deal with in this study will be

- overcoming grief

- dealing with suicide

- dealing with divorce

- dealing with sickness

- financial loss

- anger

No one gets through life without loss or grief. When we lose something of value to our lives, we experience grief. Grief is the reaction to loss. Loss does not have to always mean the death of a person; it can be anything that causes deep pain. Healthy persons who are in the Word of God deal with grief totally differently than those who do not know Him. Believers who know God in depth deal with grief entirely different than the average person. Jesus took our grief and our sorrow on the cross and when we work in that knowledge it makes such a difference.

PART ONE
Overcoming Grief

■

1. DEALING WITH GRIEF

Isaiah 53:4 KJV
Surely he hath borne our griefs, and carried our sorrows; yet we did esteem him stricken, smitten of God and afflicted.

The word '*grief*' in the Webster's II New College Dictionary means deep mental anguish as over a loss: sorrow.

Strong's 2470 Hebrew '*grief*' means to be rubbed, worn; hence to be weak, sick or afflicted from 2481 the root word means malady, anxiety, calamity, disease, grief, (is) sickness.

When we lose something of value to our lives, we can experience grief. Satan wants us to experience deep pain emotionally. Some people never allow that pain to be dealt with and this is where some get ill, angry, depressed and numerous other emotions that are not wholesome. **There needs to be a time of grieving but not too long.**

However, having said this I have heard many pray-ers say how God protected them and placed them in a bubble and they were so surrounded they did not grieve. That is the best for everyone, but not everyone is at the same level of maturity and to expect someone to try to make this happen for the sake of not showing any emotions over loss is not healthy either.

When my mother passed, I was in her room a few minutes after she passed on to Heaven.

PITIFUL or POWERFUL

My heart hurt due to her taking her last breath when I had just left the room. I had to make up my mind that I could labor in pain or get my eyes on all the good things that had happened during the time of taking care of her.

I began to weep deeply but not all from sorrow. My spirit was rejoicing that she had made it. God had just brought us through a difficult time. He kept us together and in her home which was her deepest desire. Impossibility had been made possible by God.

Even though I was praying loudly, someone listening may have thought I was in deep pain. But I was thanking God with every breath that we made it together. Even though my Mom could not hear me unless God gave her that privilege, I was talking to her and telling her just how good God was to us. Being thankful can take away many a pain and sorrow.

I was so thankful that my spirit cried out in worship with tears rolling down my face.

A 'spirit of grief' can take hold of a person and they stay in grief for many years and will not move on emotionally. This makes them pitiful instead of powerful.

The first night at home after Mom moved on to Heaven, I woke up with the feeling I had swallowed an apple and it was lodged in my throat. I recognized what it was and went into the bedroom where Mom had slept and laid across the bed and quoted the Scripture from *Isaiah 53:4*. I kept saying with tears rolling down my face, *"You took my grief and sorrows."* Each time I would quote it, the heaviness would lift a little bit more. I was very thankful to the Lord for all He had done during the year I was with her.

> *Isaiah 53:4 KJV*
> *Surely he hath borne our griefs, and carried our sorrow: yet we did esteem him stricken, smitten of God and afflicted.*

In the original Hebrew text *griefs* is sicknesses and *sorrow* is pain. **Both of these words are associated with pain. Grief is pain.**

Genesis 50:10 speaks of Joseph mourning over his father's death seven days. In the New Testament The Church has been delivered from things they did not know in the Old Testament. Walking through the change in life after death can be overwhelming **but we have the Holy Spirit inside of us. He walks with us daily and leads us through all the changes.**

In *John 11:35* Jesus' friend Lazarus died and when Jesus arrived at the house the Scripture says He wept. Then of course, we see Jesus raising him from the dead. Nevertheless **He was moved with compassion for his family, Mary and Martha.**

Compassion does not pet, stroke, or get in the ground with sickness or death, however it does care and does acts of kindness and speaks gentleness. Jesus groaned in Himself and since we know what we do about intercession, we know He had to have sensed something for Mary and Martha. He took on their need spiritually.

■■

2. TYPES OF LOSSES

There are many kinds of losses. To name a few there are some obvious ones.

Of course death, separation, or divorce. Some not so obvious can be the loss of a job, loss of funds, moving, illness (loss of health). Loss of a cherished ideal, loss of a long-term goal, loss of a pet.

Some losses are related to age such as: childhood dreams, puppy love, crushes, adolescent romances, leaving school by having to drop out of graduation, leaving home, change of jobs, loss of youth. There could be loss of beauty through an accident which scarred the face. The loss of teeth and hair may seem crazy but it does happen. Menopause, midlife crises or even retirement where your life has changed from what you have always known.

These may seem ridiculous but **these are life issues which people have to deal with. Even with children we might not realize how change can affect them.** However, living in the Epistles we have the knowledge to take the power of the blood of Jesus and minister to our children. They can be affected by changes of various kinds. Today our school system has had so many deaths due to shootings that we must learn to minister to them with the protection of Jesus. **Pleading the blood of Jesus and taking our authority completely can and will take care of these things in our lives and the lives of our family.** I remember a few years back a young woman was in the library studying and a young man came in and asked, is anyone in here a Christian? She spoke up and he shot her. This is an unusual happening; however it was a day like any other day and she probably did not think much about him asking her that question.

PITIFUL or POWERFUL

Things we might not think about, but a child getting over puppy love can be hard on them and **we need to minister to them the peace of the Lord.** If not knowing how to deal with these things spiritually a person can become really depressed. **Internalizing the pain and not allowing anyone to minister to the need can be distressing.**

This may sound silly but I remember my real first love. My Mom had forbidden me to date him any longer because she was afraid I would marry at an early age like she did and not complete my high school or do ministry. If only she had known none of that was in my mind. Her fears caused me a great deal of grief and hurt. I believe to this day the young man and I really cared for each other. I remember the day he told me the actions of your Mom toward us are causing you great trouble at home, so we should not see each other until we graduate from high school. My heart was immensely hurt. I remember how deep the wound was. A lady in our church helped me talk it out and walk through it. We did exactly as he thought we should do. At my graduation he drove over 200 miles to come and see me. We went out and talked together. When we realized each of us had taken different paths by our desires for life we broke the relationship off. However, that did not stop my heartache. He was not willing for me to continue in ministry which was my calling. However, later in life we met up again and he confided in me that he had missed God and was now fulfilling the call of God for his life. **Even though I was young I needed support to help me walk through that painful time. Parents you need to realize the pain your young person could be facing and help them walk peacefully to the other side. Listen to them and don't laugh. Pray with them and help them think it out. Help them process it.**

Other losses may be temporary loss; a child departing for college and no longer around. You may know the outcome is better and will eventually turn positive, but they can still be losses.

An unexpected dent in a new car, an argument with a friend or family member, and the next thing you know you find yourself depressed.

■ ■ ■

3. REACTIONS TO LOSS

Each loss creates an emotional wound or injury that needs to be allowed to heal.

Along with the feeling of pain, depression, and sadness, there are other reactions to loss

4

that are not so obvious such as:

- Shock or emotional numbness. It is the anesthesia that helps you through reactions to loss.

- Denial

- Bargaining (regret)

- Blaming

- Reconciliation

- Feeling helpless, fearful, empty, despairing, pessimistic, irritable, angry or restless

- Experiencing a loss of concentration, hope, motivation, and energy

- Changes in appetite, sleep patterns, or sexual drive

- Tendency to be more fatigued, error prone, and slower in speech and movement

If you recognize any of these or have experienced them, they can happen after a loss. We take a glance at these and allow God to heal them. Sometimes just to recognize what is really happening helps to dispel the pain. You know you are not going crazy but moving into healing.

■■■■

4. ROOT OF GRIEF

At the root of grief is a broken heart. I remember having to deal with a broken heart. An assistant Pastor called me forward and prayed for me. He called his wife to take me in her arms and pray over me as he had already spoken to a broken heart to be mended.

We can see from the Scripture in *Luke 4:18 KJV* that Jesus came to heal the broken hearted.

PITIFUL or POWERFUL

"The spirit of the Lord is upon me because he hath anointed me to preach the gospel to the poor; he hath sent me to heal the broken hearted, to preach deliverance to the captives, and recovering of sight to the blind, to set at liberty them that are bruised."

You see, dear one, **Jesus came to set you free from the captivity of a broken heart.** That does not mean that you will not walk through some stages of grief but the pain can be washed away by His power. He will help you walk through to the other side. Perhaps as I had already walked through many emotions by this time, but the broken heart was never spoken about before. It was the Spirit of God through the word of wisdom that got to the root of the continuing grief.

Bereavement is a wound. It is just like being very badly injured but it is on the inside. You will recover. But recovery may or may not be slow. Each person may recover at their own pace. **All the stages you walk through are meant for your healing. Little by little, you will be whole again. You will be a stronger person. Just as a broken bone knits and becomes stronger, so will you. Through the healing power of Christ your healing can be much quicker than someone who does not realize or accept what His power can do.**

Letting it go!

You must say with your own mouth, "I let it go." If we hold on to the pain, it can only get worse. If the person who passed on had done you wrong and things came out in the open what they had done, which added more shock, **you must forgive them even though they cannot hear you. You need to say it with your mouth. I let it and I let them go.**

If you say, all of this sounds good but 'that does not apply to me' or 'my case is different.' Excuses never bring deliverance. Holding on to that 'feel sorry for yourself' will never solve the hurt or pain either.

Grief will follow a pattern. It is very predictable. The phases if not walked through can delay the process of healing. There is a higher way to walk to where we are placed in a bubble above it all, but don't just expect that unless you have a supernatural thing happen for you. Not everyone experiences it that way.

The Lord walked me through the phases of grief when my husband passed. The Lord gave me hope and courage. I am a new woman. **The Lord has helped me find my true identity.**

PITIFUL or POWERFUL

One of the many Scriptures that brought me great comfort was *Isaiah 41:10*.

"Fear not, for I am with you, be not dismayed, for I am your God; I will strengthen you, I will help you. I will uphold you with my victorious right hand."

■■■■■

5. STAGES OR PHASES OF GRIEF

The number one emotion experienced is shock. Experiencing shock is a jar to the mind and the emotions then comes numbness emotionally and mentally. Shock may cause you to talk or act foolish. The following Scripture is a happening that came to David and his men. His men acted rashly and foolishly trying to take care of the pain they felt.

1 Samuel 30:1-6
1. And it came to pass, when David and his men were come to Ziklag on the third day, that the Amalekites had invaded the south, and Ziklag, and smitten Ziklag. And burned it with fire.
2. And had taken the women captives, that were therein; they slew not any, either great or small, but carried them away and went on their way.
3. So David and his men came to the city, and behold it was burned with fire and their wives, and their sons, and their daughters were taken captive.
4. Then David and all the people that were with him lifted their voice and wept, until they had not more power to weep.
5. And David's two wives were taken captives, Ahinoam the Jezreelitess, and Abigail the wife of Nabal the Carmelite.
6. And David was greatly distressed: for all the people spake of stoning him, because the soul of all the people were grieved, every man his sons and for his daughters: but David encouraged himself in the Lord.

Notice in this last verse how David dealt with the whole matter. He was being threatened by his own men. They were going to stone him. There would have been grief upon grief had they followed through with their threats. They were talking crazy. The flesh can drive us in these times, **but if we listen to our spirit like David did we will encourage ourself in the Lord.**

PITIFUL or POWERFUL

You may be numb because you are in a stage of shock. You may appear to be doing so very well. Then when everyone is gone, and you have to deal with everyday issues, you must stay in the Word of God and not isolate yourself.

- **Denial,** number two. It is hard for you to believe that this could happen to you. You know that your loved one is dead, but there is a part of the mind that resists and will not accept it. It is your mind trying to postpone the actual fact of the loss. During this stage you may have mild hallucinations that you have seen the loved one. You may have denial dreams. You may dream the loved one is still alive.

- **Anger,** number three. You become angry at your deceased loved one for not telling the doctor the problem at the first of the physical signs, angry with nurses or the physicians who cared for your loved one, with friend or relatives and some even get angry with God. (By the way, when angry with God, you are certainly angry with the wrong one.) Blaming God has caused more people to be paralyzed emotionally than any other thing.

- **Regret,** number four. You feel distress over actions either performed or unperformed before the person died. Regretting that you did not do more. Regret that you did not know what else to do. All kinds of regrets can try to greet you in the face and on your mind.

- **Blaming,** number five. You try to find someone or something to blame for your loss. You will start to think "If only I had…………….. he or she would still be here."

- **Reconciliation,** the final stage. This is when you finally bring yourself to accept what has happened.

If you recognize any of these stages I encourage you to write them down. It is not healthy to still be grieving extremely long without comfort and moving on with your life. Some grieve for months and some years. This is where the body of Christ can be such a blessing by speaking to the spirit of grief that has taken the person captive. I am not talking about missing the person or the twinges you may feel in your heart at times. I am talking about people that stay stuck in the past and cannot or do not want to move forward. *Genesis 50:10* Joseph mourned his father's death for seven days. *...and he made mourning for his father seven days.*

In *John 11:35* Jesus' friend Lazarus died and when Jesus arrived at the home the Scripture says, *He wept.* Then we see Jesus raising him from the dead. Jesus called death sleep. We need to look at it that way as well. This earth is not all the time we will get with the per-

8

son. We will see them again and spend all the time we need with them. *Jesus wept.* We all learned this as a child that it was the shortest verse in the Bible. Even though Jesus knew He was going to raise Lazarus from the dead He was moved with compassion for his family, Mary and Martha.

In *2 Samuel 12:16* We read that David had lost a child. David grieved before the child died. He laid upon the ground and would not eat. In other words, he fasted. I can only imagine the deep emotions David experienced. He had sinned and he knew it. Even though he had been forgiven he was reliving his regret I am sure. The elders tried to get him off the ground as they were concerned about him. He would not get up. On the seventh day, the child died. They feared to tell him about the death because he had been in grief so badly already. They thought his grief would be so large he would do hurt to himself. But when they whispered all around him, he perceived the child had died. (You may find people whispering around you, thinking it is too much for you to think about. But facing what happened is much healthier.) He rose up from the ground, washed and anointed himself, and changed his apparel and came in the house of the Lord and worshipped. Then he ate. His servants wanted to know why he fasted and wept while the child was still alive: but when the child died he rose up and ate. *2 Samuel 12:22* KJV *He said while the child was yet alive, I fasted and wept: for he said who can tell whether God will be gracious to me, and that the child might live? (v 23). But now he is dead, wherefore should I fast again? Can I bring him back? I shall go to him, but he shall not return to me.*

David grieved over his loss before the death of the child. Sometimes when there has been a lengthy illness the grieving process has already happened. Some people feel guilty that they are not grieving anymore. While some others looking from the outside may feel you are not caring and may judge the situation that you are glad they are gone. Let us be careful about judging lest we be judged.

Another happening with David was when he grieved over Absalom who was dividing the kingdom of Israel. He grieved so long and so strongly that he had to be corrected by the Joab the prophet. David had covered his face and cried with a loud voice, O my son Absalom, O Absalom, my son, my son! Joab came and told him he was shaming the faces of his servants, which that day had saved his life. Absalom had tried to take David's life earlier.

When parents lose a child, sometimes they grieve so long and so hard for the lost child that they ignore the living children. They lose an opportunity to allow the surviving children to share in the grieving process with them. Some parents make the surviving children feel like the child who had passed was the only child who was loved.

PITIFUL or POWERFUL

Grief is a funny thing. David should have been glad to some degree because the boy was a heartache. The servants had saved the lives of his whole family. Joab told him that if Absalom had lived and we had all died, then it had pleased you well. So he was told to rise up and speak comfortably with his servants. If you do not rise up and go forth, they will not stay one more night with you. And that will be worse than any evil that you have already experienced from your youth until now. So David rose up and sat in the gate of the city and all the people came by. They had already fled to their tents.

I have seen people who grieved so long that no one wanted to be around them. This is what David was experiencing in *2 Samuel 19:1-8*.

Grief has no timetable unless we set one. Since feelings of grief can be unpredictable focus on the following Scriptures.

> *Isaiah 53:4-5 KJV*
> *4. Surely he hath borne our griefs, and carried our sorrows; yet we did esteem him stricken, smitten of God and afflicted.*
> *5. But he was wounded (tormented) for our transgressions. He was bruised for our iniquities: the chastisement of our peace was upon Him and by His stripes we are healed.*

> *1 Thessalonians 4:13-14 KJV*
> *13. But I would not have you to be ignorant brethren, concerning them which are asleep that ye sorrow not, even as others which have no hope.*
> *14. For if we believe that Jesus died and rose again, even so them also which sleep in Jesus will God bring with Him.*

Meditate on these Scriptures and allow them to bring comfort and healing.

Grief has a way of trying to follow you wherever you go. I was with a friend and we were seeking God concerning answers to my husband's death. We felt we needed to go away and change our environment. We went to a city that had wonderful Christian Entertainment.

When we arrived in our hotel room, I began to cry. Nothing that we had done should have reminded me of my husband. He and I had not been to that city together. We prayed through the feeling of grief that had tried to overtake me. I have found it is very helpful to have someone strong in faith to help you walk through a crisis.

PITIFUL or POWERFUL

The loss of a spouse is very difficult. You were one in the flesh and you sense that half of you has gone somewhere. Life will not be the same. You will be faced with newness on every front. You will have to make decisions that no one else can make but you. You will have to decide whether to continue to live where the two of you lived etc.

These decisions cannot be made out of guilt or trying to do what you feel the deceased person would want you to do. If you do not do what you feel you should do, you will not be happy. If we are not careful, the way we feel will affect our decisions. We must learn to lean on the leading of the Holy Spirit to direct us daily.

It is good to list any major decisions you are facing. Ask the Holy Spirit to help you with each of these decisions. He is more than able and more than willing to help you, comfort you and lead you.

I had always heard that you should not make any major decisions for one year after a husband of wife's departure from this life. In my case I had to rise up and make major decisions every day. For me, the sooner I was involved in the decisions the better off I was. We need to do everything for ourselves that we can. It is great to have help. There were things that I thank my daughter and her husband for doing that made all the other things I had to deal with much easier. But dealing with the decisions and making them yourself keeps you healthy mentally. As you can see there are no set answers, we are each unique.

If you find photographs of memories help you in the grieving process, use them. After a while if you feel they are binding you to a dead past, get rid of them or set them aside. If you plan to remarry the best thing you can do is to take the photos and place them where they are not in front of you and your new spouse. Box them up, store them, or give them away to your children. You must accept the fact that the loved one is gone and start making a new life for yourself. Their memory will always live in your heart.

Relationships will change

You will have to be open to new relationships. Some of your relationships in the past will change. Some people you will not be comfortable being with as they are couples and now you are alone. Not all situations will be this way as some people are loyal to you as a couple. Going out to dinner when everyone is a couple and you are alone can be a bit hurtful. I found I have to tell myself they love you and enjoy your company, so relax and enjoy seeing them enjoy their life.

PITIFUL or POWERFUL

Sensing death near you

In observing, sometimes the person(s) left behind get sick after a divorce or death. Statistics tell us that anywhere from 2 to 5 years after a death the other spouse left will become ill. Now I know that does not have to happen. I have a ministry called, WIDOWS WITH PURPOSE. I love including WIDOWERS as well in this ministry. If we find our purpose of life, the chances are our health can and will become better and we will thrive and not just survive. When my husband passed, I could sense death nearby me. I felt it was trying to take me. I fought it with the words of my mouth. *"I will live and not die and declare the wondrous works of my Lord."* I have not just survived. I have thrived.

Children and Grief

If a child is involved in the grieving with you, it is very important that you encourage them to talk to you about what they are feeling. Children have a tendency to blame themselves for the death of a loved one. They may feel like they should have been a better child or perhaps they were angry with the person, wished they would go away, or even wished they were dead. They will feel that what they said or thought is what caused the person to die. Whatever you do, do not pile guilt upon them.

Make sure that you are not so caught up in your own grief that you forget about the child. Do not make the mistake of allowing them to internalize what they are feeling. Be sure that you draw your children out and talk to them. Never laugh or make light of anything they tell you they are feeling. Spend lots of time praying with them, loving on them, listening to them, and allowing them to be children.

Tell them you miss the person. Be honest with them. Tell them if you feel frightened or afraid, but don't leave it there. Pray together for each other. Read Scriptures to them. *2 Timothy 1:4* Paul was talking to Timothy. He told him he was mindful of his tears, but that he wanted him filled with joy. Then he began to prophesy to him. He built him up. He reminded him about his mother and his grandmother and their faith they had taught him. He told him to stir up the gift of God in Him. Paul pointed out to him the remembrance of the time when hands were laid on him and gifts from God were imparted into his life. Encourage the child and bring good memories out to them. *2 Timothy 1:7* is a verse we hear a lot. *For God has not given us a spirit of fear; but of power, and of love and of a sound mind.* Paul was encouraging Timothy to be restored in joy. He was speaking against *fear* and called it a spirit. We must remember we have power over evil spirits in

Jesus Name. Since fear is a spirit, we must speak to that spirit and tell it to leave; that we have the mind of Christ.

Luke 10:19
Behold, I give unto you power to tread on serpents and scorpions and over all the power of the enemy and nothing shall by any means harm you.

Often a child is afraid that you or they are next in line to die. Their fear has to be addressed and not ignored. Bring comfort to them. Introduce them to Jesus and how much He cares for them. He left the Holy Spirit here on the earth to bring comfort to us.

John 16:7
Nevertheless I tell you the truth; it is expedient for you that I go away: for if I go not away, the Comforter will not come unto you, but if I depart, I will send him unto you.

Then talk about Heaven. Learn all you can about the subject of Heaven. Read books where people have visited Heaven and came back to tell their story. Make sure they are spirit-filled books and not new age mystic things. This is an opportunity for you and the child to grow together in the Lord. *'Heaven is For Real'* by Todd Burpo and Lynn Vincent is one title helpful for a child.

■■■■■■
6. DEALING WITH SUICIDE

While this chapter could be very heavy for me I choose not to allow it to be. I have experienced it but have been healed of all the ramifications it tried to leave for my life. Shame tried to come on me. Inadequacy tried to take me down. Questions of why and how could this happen to me, a Spirit-filled person who prayed daily and took my place in God, how could this happen? I experienced various emotions that I had to rise up above and win over them.

My husband was seeing a godly counselor at my insistence as I could see he was having emotional outbursts that were getting worse. He was getting sick mentally and it was very distressing to live with. If I had not had the Holy Spirit as my helper I don't know how I could have done it. I spent much time in intercessory prayer for him. I felt like a failure in prayer. The Holy Spirit had showed my friend who was assisting us in the ministry that he planned to take his life. She did not know he had attempted it two other times. We prayed and shared this information with the counselor. He denied that he even had such thoughts. Before you might think or say if you had not said it with your mouth it would not have happened. I want to say, God does tell us things in prayer and warns us about them. We can either stop them through prayer or He will get us prepared to walk through them. I pled with my husband to get help. He was in denial and would not accept any counsel. It was a very precarious and dangerous situation. We shared what we had picked up in prayer with the counselor but my husband said we were just imagining these things. He said he had no intentions of ever taking his life. When he was the most emphatic, it was the next day he took his life.

In warning me, the Holy Spirit told me to be real sweet to him. He told me to have no regrets. He also told me to release him and let the Lord have him. I obeyed the Lord in the face of some things that could have made me very angry and cause me to lash out at him. I would have regretted that kind of behavior and the Lord had prompted me to not have any regrets. God's instructions to me were: you stay sweet no matter how he acts or what he does. I am so grateful that I obeyed God.

The counselor spoke with my husband numerous times but on the occasion where it is very important he told the counselor that it was all a figment of my imagination and he had no intention of taking his life. He promised the counselor that he would call him before he would harm himself in any way. The very next morning he took his life.

If you have had anyone in your life commit suicide I can feel exactly what you feel. Many have asked me how he did it. I know they mean well and while I can speak of it freely without pain today, I choose not to in many cases. I never want to give the enemy any opportunity to bring shame or victim feelings on me. Satan does not like us at all. He wants to keep us from knowing who we are. An evil spirit had taken control of my husband's mind and I will not glorify anything he does. I will glorify God Who has brought me safely through it and kept my sanity.

Sometimes an individual becomes so mentally and emotionally ill they will not allow anyone to help them. Whenever the counselor would be directed by the Holy Spirit how to help him in an area, he would clam up, resist and become angry. Everything was in place for my husband to have complete deliverance but he would not accept it. God has given us free will and He will not violate our wills. We must be careful what we yield our wills to.

PITIFUL or POWERFUL

After his death a family member shared with me just how bad his life had been as a child. My heart ached for him and I cried out, "why didn't you tell me?" I picked up things in my spirit and would say, some things happened to you that were not good would you please talk with me about it? He would never come close to sharing it. He may have been threatened that if he ever told something bad would come upon him. I have no way of knowing since all family members are gone now. I had the sense that he was threatened that if he ever told family secrets things would not be good for him.

My husband had come to Jesus as a boy. Due to all the things he suffered in his life, his soul was very ill. It hurt me to know we were in anointed, spirit-filled meetings and he never allowed the Holy Spirit to touch his soul (mind, will and emotions). The pain and hurt was so intense that he wanted to escape rather than to face it.

So many people told me he is in hell. I heard that more than once. Not being indifferent but to try to shut them up, I would say, *"If he is, there is nothing I can do about it now."* How harsh to go about telling people those kind of words. You don't know and neither do I. God knows hearts and we don't. Those words are not comforting to a family member that is dealing with a death of this sort.

I cried out to God and He led me to Scriptures that helped me tremendously. I do not advocate suicide. To me it is one of the most selfish things a person can do. The people they leave behind to go on are hurt and are left with scars unless they know the Lord and His healing power. I will share the following Scriptures to help anyone who needs comfort.

In *Judges 16:28-31* Samson brought the pillars in on himself. He had a goal in mind to spare the Children of Israel from the Philistines. However, he took them all out including himself. *Samson* means Joy. His destiny was to bring joy, but through yielding to his flesh through the temptation of a heathen woman he brought great grief to himself, to the nation, and to his family. He lost out on his destiny through his choice. So often people who are called of God to accomplish great things fail to do so because they yield to their flesh rather than what God has in mind for them. While attending Bible College one of my professors made the statement that yielding to the flesh was more dangerous than yielding to a demon. I had to digest that one in thought for some time. When I realized what he was saying I realized how dangerous it is to allow the flesh to reign and take us in. In Samson's case it was the most deadly decision he could have made. **Samson had a lot of time to repent while in prison. Even with all that Samson did to cause such grief, the Bible mentions him in the Faith Hall of Fame in *Hebrews 11:32.***

PITIFUL or POWERFUL

Read *1 Samuel 28:3-19*

Samuel was dead, and buried in his own city, Ramah. Saul was preparing to lead the people of Israel to battle with the Philistines. When Saul saw the size of the Philistine army he was so filled with fear that his heart trembled. He kept talking to God, but God would not answer him, so he decided to see a woman with a familiar spirit. He had disobeyed God and done many things that God was not pleased with him about. So he took matters in his own hands. Saul had passed a law that witches, people with familiar spirits, and wizards were not allowed to practice in the land of Israel. Saul was told there was a woman in Endor who had a familiar spirit. He disguised himself and went to see the woman. Saul told her to call up Samuel. When Saul perceived that she had brought up Samuel, he did not like what he heard from him. He told Saul how the Lord had withdrawn himself from him. In verse 19 he received the words that his heart had trembled over. *Moreover the Lord will also deliver Israel with thee into the hand of the Philistines: and tomorrow shalt thou and thy sons shall be with me: the Lord also shall deliver the host of Israel into the hand of the Philistines.*

In *1 Samuel 31:4* we find that Saul fell on his own sword. He and his sons died in battle. Samuel had told him that he and his sons would be with him tomorrow.

I do not believe that every person who commits suicide is in Heaven. I believe that just like Samson and Saul some will be there. We are spirit, soul and body and some people are very sick in their soul. Yes, God can and will heal them if they will allow him to.

We need to tell those whose family member or loved one has taken their life, there are some things that we will find out at the end of life. They are secret things and they belong to the Lord. To tell everyone a pat answer that they will see their loved one in Heaven is the same as telling them they are going to hell. We need not to try to be their answer. Encourage them to speak to the Lord about what has happened and receive their healing of the pain it has caused. We should minister to them in the love of God. They need our love. Their loved one for whatever reason was sick in their soul and perhaps as well as their bodies and they were unable to accept God's healing power through Christ.

Brother Kenneth E. Hagin, Sr. told how his mother had a nervous breakdown. His father deserted them when he was young. He was a very sick young man as well. All of these pressures of life stacked up and they were too much for his mother. She snapped and attempted suicide. He had questions and the Holy Spirit showed him the Spirit, Soul and Body revelation.

16

PITIFUL or POWERFUL

1 Thessalonians 5:23
And the very God of peace sanctify you wholly; and I pray God your whole spirit and soul and body be preserved blameless unto the coming of our Lord Jesus Christ.

He asked the Lord if she had committed suicide, would she have gone to hell. The Holy Spirit showed him she would have gone to Heaven. The Holy Spirit showed him that she was mentally ill, which is a sickness of the soul. If a person were sick in their body and died, we expect them to make it to Heaven. If a person is sick in their mind and emotions, they are just as ill as a person who is physically ill.

THIS IS NOT GIVING ANYONE A LICENSE TO COMMIT SUICIDE.

God is the only One Who knows when a person is truly mentally ill. Only God can read the heart. I do know this for a fact; there is no problem that God cannot help us through. Pressures of life can try to make a person think, there is no answer, but there is in Christ.

The person who took their life almost always leaves many unanswered questions. They usually leave the family feeling horrible guilt. The suicidal person is not thinking correctly and they leave things that puzzle you even more, or they take the secrets to the grave with them. We are the ones who have to get it resolved with God.

God has walked me through all the stages and brought me into deep healing. He has given me a new anointing even though the enemy wanted to take everything from me and my family. Keep your eyes fixed upon the Lord and His power and healing for your emotions will come.

■■■■■■■

7. SUICIDAL THOUGHTS

If you are entertaining thoughts of suicide, allow me to say this to you. Have you ever thought God has such great plans for you and the devil is trying to talk you out of it? To combat thoughts of suicide, you must take the Word of God and combat them. You must not fear to speak to satan and tell him you are not listening to him anymore.

PITIFUL or POWERFUL

Jeremiah 29:11 says, *"God's plans are for good and not for evil."* Speaking to the forces of darkness the opposite of what they are bombarding you with, will make the change in your thinking. Say, *"I am God's masterpiece."*

I heard a minister say, *"Tough times don't last but tough people do."* You can make it.

The following prayer is important to pray out loud.

Thoughts of suicide, I will not entertain you. Devil, I speak to you to shut up! Get out of me now! You are evil and destructive! I will not allow you to take me out by my own hands. Spirit of suicide go in Jesus' Name. I say, "God has plans for me for good and I will not die but live and declare the wonderful works of the Lord."

Go to www.rjim.org and write us and we will pray for you and guide you to more help in overcoming these thoughts.

For immediate help call Dr. Joyce Brown 1-800-675-1777 Suicide Prevention.

PART TWO
Surviving Divorce

■

1. DEALING WITH DIVORCE

I want to start this chapter by telling you, God hates divorce but He loves the divorced person.

I believe one of the hardest things to deal with is a divorce. The hardest thing to do is letting go. You and the other person have a history together. It is like a living death. The person keeps surfacing and in many cases continues to try to do damage or be vindictive. If children are involved it is even harder. There are deep feelings that need to be dealt with. Some people use the children to try to get revenge or to try and hold on to the other person. Don't do it and do not allow it to be done to you.

Philippians 3:13 KJV
Brethren, I count not myself to have apprehended but this one thing I do, forgetting those things, which are behind, and reaching forth unto those things which are before.

Isaiah 43:15-19 KJV
15. I am the Lord, Your Holy One, the creator of Israel, your king.
16. Thus saith the Lord, which maketh a way in the sea and a path in the mighty waters.
17. Which bringeth forth the chariot and horse, the army and the power; they shall lie down together, they shall not rise: they are extinct, they are quenched as tow.
18. Remember ye not the former thing; neither consider the things of old.
19. Behold, I will do a new thing now it shall spring forth shall ye not know it? I will

even make a way in the wilderness, and rivers in the desert.

These Scriptures may seem like they are impossible for a person to keep, but I believe when the Word of God is applied to our lives it works and it accomplishes what it is sent out to do. God will heal the hurt.

One of the things that tries to follow divorce is shame. Shame tries to come with suicide and divorce; any kind of trauma or pain the enemy loves to pile on shame. The Church used to not know how to deal with divorced people. Too many times they were outcast without any help or support. Thank God today we have support teams of people who know just how to handle the situation and help those who so desperately need the support emotionally and even financially.

I want to quote **Dr. Don Colbert** from his book **'Deadly Emotions'**, *"Shame is a truly toxic emotion."*

Shame is the reflection onto the victim of an abuser's bad behavior. Many children who bear the burden of shame carry their misery into adulthood. Adults who have deeply internalized shame after fear intimacy and bring commitment problems into marriage relationships. They struggle to maintain a marriage. Sometimes drifting from marriage to marriage and from breakup to breakup, never quite able to see their own self-sabotaging behaviors as associated with the shame they carry like a giant, invisible weight deep within. Deep down the shamed person feels he is genuinely unlovable and unworthy of anyone's care.

Recognizing the shame and bringing it before the Lord for healing is the answer and will go deep in the emotions and relieve the pressure of shame. When that happens being set free can give a peaceable life. The mind has to be renewed with the Word of God that they are bearing something Jesus has already taken.

■■

2. LETTING GO

When you have gone through a divorce you may experience some or all of the following losses. Read the losses, and write the ones you have experienced, and add any that are not mentioned. When I wrote the losses of divorce, some may have happened to you and some may not have. In no way am I wishing you to focus on the losses and forget who you are in Christ. The big secret of overcoming is staying focused on restoration in every area. Satan is the destroyer. *(John 10:10)*. He is the one who enters into homes and tries to destroy relationships. Remember who the enemy is and get all the knowledge you can about how to take your place of authority for your family. I want to encourage you to read *"The Believer's Authority" by Kenneth E. Hagin.* His life was changed in his early years of ministry by reading *"The Authority of the Believer" by John A. MacMillan.*

Both books are life-changing. What we enlarge is enlarged. Therefore, we must enlarge the Word of God against all these possible losses named here. There is Scripture to fight against every single one of these losses.

- **Loss of self-acceptance.** The rejection of a spouse can make us feel that we are unacceptable, don't fit in, don't matter, are unimportant, and of little value. Ever since Adam and Eve were rejected from the Garden of Eden, we have all been searching for permanent acceptance.

Recognize the pain of rejection and take authority over it in Jesus Name.

CONFESSION: "I am accepted in Christ, no evil spirit can reign in my life. I choose to believe I am accepted and not rejected. I do not allow rejection to take hold of me. I take my place with Christ seated with Him in the heavenly realm." *[Ephesians 2:4-6]*

- **Loss of love.** Love is the deepest level of acceptance. When you are divorced it seems as though the world knows that your spouse does not love you. It does not seem to matter to you that family and friends love you, the love of your life is gone.

God wants to restore you to a better place.

The meaning of being restored is to make alive, to turn back, to make whole and complete, to make thoroughly right.

Satan, I take my place in God and the loss of love in my life is a lie. Someone loves me more than I could ever believe, His Name is Jesus Christ. I accept His love into my heart fully. I am loved, accepted, and respected through all He has done for me.

PITIFUL or POWERFUL

■ **Loss of self-esteem.** If you have no doubt about who you are in Christ and you know all you did to try and make your marriage work, loss of self-esteem is minimal. For some, though, the shame, guilt, and regret may eat away at you. When a spouse leaves you, either emotionally or physically, it is common, for you to feel as if you are not attractive, lovable and desirable; even if you know you are.

CONFESSION:
Psalms 139:14 YLT
I confess Thee, because that with wonders I have been distinguished. Wonderful are Thy works, And my soul is knowing it well.

■ **Loss of sense of belonging.** You and your spouse created and were part of a whole family unit, and now you are not. Divorce can leave you feeling totally disconnected.

CONFESSION:
Song of Solomon 2:4 KJV
He brought me to the banqueting house, and His banner over me was love.

Song of Solomon 2:4 AMP
He brought me to the banqueting house and his banner over me was love [for love waved as a protecting and comforting banner over our head when I was near him.]

■ **Loss of your husband or wife.** You and your spouse became "one flesh." A husband and wife are intended to be part of each other, spiritually, emotionally, sexually, and physically. Now that part of you is gone and you have no control over it.

Song of Solomon 2:16 KJV
My beloved is mine, and I am his: he feedeth among the lilies.

Colossians 2:10 KJV
And ye are complete in Him which is the head of all principality and power.

Matthew 28:20b
...lo, I am with you alway even to the end of world. Amen!

CONFESSION: "I am complete in Christ and have authority over principalities and powers in His Name. *No weapon formed again me shall prosper.*

I am complete in Him. GLORY!"

- **Loss of your lover.** You no longer have a lover to hold you, love you, caress you, or play with and tease you. No one to satisfy you emotionally, physically or sexually.

Colossians 1:4 AMPC
For we have heard of your faith in Christ Jesus [the leaning of your entire human personality on Him in absolute trust and confidence in His power, wisdom, and goodness] and of the love which you [have and show] for all the saints (God's consecrated ones).

This is what faith is: leaning of your entire personality on God. Let Him heal you and guide your life.

He is the author and finisher of your faith.

Hebrews 12:2 KJV
Looking unto Jesus the author and finisher of our faith; who for the joy that was set before him endured the cross, despising the shame, and is set down at the right hand of the throne of God.

CONFESSION: "I lean my whole personality on Him. I have trust and confidence in His power. I am full of His wisdom and goodness. He is the author and finisher of my faith. GLORY!"

- **Loss of someone to love.** Loving someone is as important as having someone love you.

If you have lost love, you need to show forth love to others who are hurting as well as you are. Look around and don't focus just on your need. It is very healing to help someone else. The tendency is to be so engulfed in your own need that it is blinding to anyone else's. But it is the road out of grief. The tendency can also be to be together with hurting people and wallow in each other's hurt. If you do this, neither of you make any progress.

Luke 6:38 KJV
Give, and it shall be given unto you; good measure, pressed down, shaken together, and running over, shall men give into your bosom.

PITIFUL or POWERFUL

CONFESSION: "I am an overcomer by the power invested in me by Jesus Christ. I refuse to live in a self-pity state and wallow in it with others. I minister in love to them with understanding of their need, but I do not amplify it by rehearsing mine."

▪ **Loss of your provider.** Even if you were the major breadwinner, your spouse probably contributed to your lifestyle financially or took care of many household needs. Now you are on your own.

Philippians 4:19 NIV
And my God will meet all your needs according to the riches of his glory in Christ Jesus.

2 Corinthians 8:14 NIV
At the present time your plenty will supply what they need, so that in turn their plenty will supply what you need. The goal is equality,

Psalms 23:1 NIV
The Lord is my shepherd, I lack nothing.

James 1:4 AMP
And let endurance have its perfect result and do a thorough work, so that you may be perfect and completely developed [in your faith], lacking in nothing.

CONFESSION: "I choose to believe that God is my source of supply. He provides for me no matter what my status in life is. I look to Him and not to man. He takes me by the hand and leads me into a new way of living in His plan. GLORY!"

▪ **Loss of a partner.** You no longer have someone waiting for you when you come home. No one to share the events of the day with, laugh, or to cry with. Genuine fellowship is missing.

I had an experience that may help you. I was at my Mom's home helping her. I know she had said to me many times I am so lonely, I feel lost. When she went to the hospital due to a fall, I was in her house alone. A sensation of being so lost came over me. I felt like my insides were to burst with crying and feeling lost. When I would get away from the house it would lift. I got in her car to drive to my daughter's home to try to get some relief. I thought I had gotten overly tired and needed to get away. While I was in the car

PITIFUL or POWERFUL

driving to her home, I began to seek God about this overwhelming thing. He impressed on me, you are feeling just what your Mom has been dealing with. My Mom prayed in the spirit a lot so it surprised me to hear this was what she was dealing with. I began to pray for her to be released from this. I also prayed for her house to be freed of this loneliness spirit. Then intercessory prayer came on me and He told me this is what so many others are feeling and they have no one to help them get out of it. I stood in the gap for many people that day. As I did it lifted. When I got back to her home I told the spirits of darkness to leave in Jesus Name.

I believe if we give into the loneliness and keep living that way, a demonic presence gets in on it and makes it overwhelming. Demonic presences have their own grief due to their fall and they love to project that to people. It gives them satisfaction to see you lost and lonely. Many a person has taken their own life due to the loneliness. They don't seem to know how to get past it. But if you are a believer, let God lead you on how to handle this. Occupy your mind with other things and read the Word of God out loud to yourself.

John 14:18 AMP
"I will not leave you as orphans [comfortless, bereaved, and helpless]; I will come [back] to you.

Psalms 46:1-3 AMP
1. God is our refuge and strength [mighty and impenetrable], A very present and well-proved help in trouble.
2. Therefore we will not fear, though the earth should change. And though the mountains be shaken and slip into the heart of the seas,
3. Though its waters roar and foam, Though the mountains tremble at its roaring. Selah.

CONFESSION: "God is my refuge. No demonic presence is welcome around me. He never leaves me bereaved, lonely and helpless. He is my present help in time of trouble. I lend myself to mind renewal. I fellowship with the King of Kings. GLORY!"

▪ **Loss of companionship.** You have lost your TV partner. You now go to the movies alone and eat all your meals alone.

Invite the Lord to dinner. Set a lovely table. Be careful what you watch on TV. Be careful not to watch anything that leads to depression or upset. The enemy will take you back to memories that lead to self-pity. The hole will get deeper and you have to climb back out

PITIFUL or POWERFUL

and it is harder to get out. If you watch things that lead you down a wrong path that is like pulling your own hair. Move away from those things that are not enhancing your life.

One of the things I did when my husband died was watch movies where people overcame against all odds. I watched true stories where the people won over all kinds of adversity.

Colossians 2:10 AMP
And in Him you have been made complete [achieving spiritual stature through Christ], and He is the head over all rule and authority [of every angelic and earthly power].

Ephesians 3:18-19 AMP
18. be fully capable of comprehending with all the saints (God's people) the width and length and height and depth of His love [fully experiencing that amazing, endless love]; 19. and [that you may come] to know [practically, through personal experience] the love of Christ which far surpasses [mere] knowledge [without experience], that you may be filled up [throughout your being] to all the fullness of God [so that you may have the richest experience of God's presence in your lives, completely filled and flooded with God Himself].

CONFESSION: "I am complete in Him. I comprehend God's love. I have the personal experience of loving the Lord. His love surpasses me and fills my very being. I am completely flooded with God Himself. GLORY!"

▪ **Loss of your children.** One spouse may lose custody of their children. You lose large chunks of time because of visitation schedules.

Psalms 23:3 KJV
He restoreth my soul: he leadeth me in the paths of righteousness for his name's sake.

Psalms 51:12 KJV
Restore unto me the joy of thy salvation; and uphold me with thy free spirit

Always keep in mind that restoring is in God's nature. Damage may be done by the parent with custody by trying to sway the children another way, but remember if you have placed the Word of God in them, their spirit man will be spoken to by the Lord. You must not fear and speak the Word of God. These kinds of things can bring great anxiety. You have to refuse the anxiousness that arises at the moment it comes. If you pray in tongues keep on pressing through in tongues. God will lift you above all the attacks of the enemy.

26

PITIFUL or POWERFUL

■ **Loss of your children's loyalty.** In an intact family, children usually don't take sides. They might "betray" you by acting as a spy for the other parent, or in other ways.

In most cases of divorce children are very confused. They love both parents. When one speaks against the other one, it is even more confusing. The best thing you can do is express any concerns if there is danger of any kind, but to tell the child all your mate's faults really puts the children in a bad spot. Even those concerns may need to be spoken to a third party and prayed over. Let God lead you.

I have known cases with children where one parent completely took the children out of the other one's life. The one it happened to was not speaking against the other mate. We stood together (3 of us) in agreement that restoration would come with the children. It was heartbreaking, but we had to keep our eyes on the Lord's Word. Today I can say the relationship is restored. It takes time but you cannot waver during the process. Find a Scripture to stand on. Let God send you His Word. If you ask Him, He will. It could come in a sermon, a broadcast or quiet time with Him. Your spirit will know that is His Word. You take it like God spoke it in an audible voice to you. It is yours and don't let it go.

Proverbs 26:20-21 AMP
20. For lack of wood the fire goes out, And where there is no whisperer [who gossips], contention quiets down.
21. Like charcoal to hot embers and wood to fire, So is a contentious man to kindle strife.

■ **Loss of control over your children.** When they are with the other spouse you have no control over what they see, hear, or do. It can be scary. What does the other spouse tell them about you?

If the other mate is vindictive and speaks ugly about you, you must cover yourself and your children with the blood of Jesus. Pray over them before they leave the house. If you have usually been praying with them already they won't think much about it. If you have not, they may ask questions. So be wise in your words to them. Pray God's best for them and protection over them. Be a comfort to your child when they return home.

Fear has torment and gives the enemy an inroad into our lives. Take hold of the fear and anxiety trying to hinder you at all times. If you can take authority over the fear, then nothing shall hinder you. God is peaceful and you give Him power to work on your case. Cover yourself from vicious words.

PITIFUL or POWERFUL

Philippians 4:6-7 KJV
6. Be careful for nothing; but in every thing by prayer and supplication with thanksgiving let your requests be made known unto God.
7. And the peace of God, which passeth all understanding, shall keep your hearts and minds through Christ Jesus.

Isaiah 26:3 NASB
The steadfast of mind You will keep in perfect peace, Because he trusts in You.

■ **Loss of financial security.** Income is halved, pensions are split, and retirement funds are drained for attorney's fees.

Sometimes you fear that you will never recover financially and are doomed to poverty for life. But I have to tell you Jesus is the redeemer and restorer and brings life back and if you are faithful to Him and keep on giving and tithing, He will redeem you.

Everyday walk out your life with Him. Tell Him He is your source and you choose to believe that no person can hinder you financially. Financial support is from Him and He alone works wonders to perform for you. Keep focused on Him.

Proverbs 11:24 NKJV
There is one who scatters, yet increases more; And there is one who withholds more than is right, But it leads to poverty.

Proverbs 10:22 NIV
The blessing of the LORD brings wealth, without painful toil for it.

Whatever you do, stay under the blessing by staying out of strife, contention, maliciousness or hatefulness.

CONFESSION: "I choose to be a tither and giver regardless of my circumstances. I will not fear financially what man can do to me. You, Lord are my source. You will never forsake me nor let me run out of bread, clothing or daily necessities. I trust in You no matter what destruction is trying to come to my bank account, my checkbook, or my everyday living. I will not allow bitterness to rise up inside of me. I keep myself free in Christ and He will take care of me. GLORY TO GOD!"

■ **Loss of time.** Now when you come home from work, you have to handle everything by yourself. You don't have the time for the rest, fun, friends, prayer, reading, and recreation necessary for a balanced life.

I say keep prayer and Bible reading first and all else will come in line miraculously.

Matthew 6:33 NIV
But seek first his kingdom and his righteousness, and all these things will be given to you as well.

Matthew 6:33 NLT
Seek the Kingdom of God above all else, and live righteously, and he will give you everything you need.

In the book of Nehemiah, God gave an assignment to Nehemiah to rebuild the walls of Jerusalem. God gave him, the king, queen and others to help him in this assignment. Here are Nehemiah's words: *"The generous hand of my God was with me in this and the king gave them to me." Nehemiah 2:4-9a*

I suggest you read all of these verses. *4-9a of Nehemiah.*

CONFESSION: "I seek God above all else. His mercy shines on me. He gives me amply all I need in time, health, peace, friends, etc... He guides me with His eye and I give my time to Him first and He sends help in all areas of my life. I trust in Him to help me to be healthy in spirit, soul and body. He sends help on every side to help me in His presence abide. In Him and His blessings I have taken inside and there I choose to abide. Heaviness is removed from me. I have cast it all on Him. GLORY TO GOD!"

■ **Loss of home.** Do you miss your big kitchen and dining room and the lovely yard? Maybe you miss having a laundry room with a washer and dryer in your house.

Valuing peace above everything else means more than a house, a yard, and all the necessities of life. While these things are temporal and mean a lot to our everyday soul, we must remember who lives inside of us. Self-pity will rob you of your strength, energy and eventually your health. God has promised in His Word if we will seek His Kingdom first, all these things will be added unto us. Remember to speak to the Lord in fellowship about every single thing, He knows how to manage to bless you beyond measure.

PITIFUL or POWERFUL

Say this out loud. "Wealth and riches are in my house."

Psalms 112:3S KJV
Wealth and riches shall be in his house: and his righteousness endureth forever.

John 16:33 NIV
"I have told you these things, so that in me you may have peace. In this world you will have trouble. But take heart! I have overcome the world."

CONFESSION: "My God supplies for me all that I need in my spirit, soul and body. He knows my likes and my dislikes. He knows about my washing machine, my dryer, my yard and all I may miss. I choose to abide in peace and trust God for all things being added to me. I am not of this world system but in a Heavenly Kingdom and therefore nothing holds me back. HALLELUJAH!"

▪ **Loss of good credit.** Loss of financial stability seems like a loss of power over your own life.

Going through a credit instability is not good. However, if we determine in our newness of life to trust God and not lean on credit, we will come into more prosperity than we have known before.

Psalms 25:2-3 NIV
2. I trust in you; do not let me be put to shame, nor let my enemies triumph over me.
3. No one who hopes in you will ever be put to shame, but shame will come on those who are treacherous without cause.

All that Satan has stolen from you is replaceable.

Proverbs 6:30-31 NIV
30. People do not despise a thief if he steals to satisfy his hunger when he is starving.
31. Yet if he is caught, he must pay sevenfold, though it costs him all the wealth of his house.

CONFESSION: "I trust in God and not in uncertain riches. My God is my restorer of my reputation. I choose not to be ashamed but lifted up above all disaster, shame and lack. None of these things belong to me and they have an expiration date. I choose to believe that date is up. I have a new day in Christ and nothing will hinder me or hold me down or back. The thief has been found out and he has to repay seven times all things to me in Jesus Name! GLORY TO GOD!"

- **Loss of friends and relatives.** You lose friendships with your spouse's former friends and their family. You will find various relationships will end because of divorce.

Not only do we grieve the loss of the mate, but the loss of friendships can also loom over us trying to make us grieve. Sometimes relatives on both sides misunderstand and they will disregard your feelings about holidays and other family celebrations. The best thing you can do for yourself if you are left out is to make your own plans. Plan a different time than you normally would have with their family. For instance, if it is Christmas make plans to celebrate a different day of that week with the family. The biggest mistake you can make is sit around lonely doing nothing and expect people to come to you. You have to make a new life and a new way of doing things.

Isaiah 43:18-19 NIV
18. "Forget the former things; do not dwell on the past.
19. See, I am doing a new thing! Now it springs up; do you not perceive it?
I am making a way in the wilderness and streams in the wasteland."

CONFESSION: "I choose not to remember the former things. They are gone and I have forgiven those who have hurt me. I choose a joyful path God has for me. I gather people by His Spirit unto myself and make a new life of peace and celebration. My heart may hurt but I choose to release the sorrow and let Him heal all my wounds. It is a new day of freshness and I have God's wisdom working in me on making a new life. GLORY!"

- **Loss of family approval and acceptance.** Maybe your parents really liked your 'ex' or are angry that you put the kids through this. Many times you find yourself under attack by relatives.

Prepare yourself that the person may show up at family celebrations. You have to decide what you will or won't do. Just count the cost of your decision before you make it. Rejection does not belong to us. Every one of us can have a sting of rejection at times, but getting quiet and forgiving the person and asking God to bless them and bless them yourself can take away the sting of the rejection.

CONFESSION: "I choose to release all those who misunderstand the motives of my heart. Reveal to them anything they need to know. I let go of those relatives who speak words of attack to me. They cannot possibly know all that I know about the situation. The Lord helps me to go forth and I take authority over the ugly words spoken to and about me. For in Christ I am free indeed. I am accepted in the beloved, Jesus Christ. GLORY TO GOD!"

Ephesians 1:6 KJV
To the praise of the glory of his grace, wherein he hath made us accepted in the be-loved.

▪ **Loss of role in your church.** Did you belong to a couples or married group at church?

The best way to deal with this feeling of being displaced, is to search for a place to be a blessing to someone else. If you feel it is right to join a single's group in the church, talk to the director of that ministry and find a place. If not there, then join something else to take up the slack. Today churches are more helpful than they used to be to the divorced person. They used to reject you. In some places that may still be true. If your ex is in that church and stays there, you may need to ask the Lord for direction. Speak to your pastor about your situation. Whatever you do, don't become isolated for long lengths of time. Stay connected to people.

CONFESSION: "I have divine connections. God makes me prosper with true friends. He helps me with my family and church family making celebrations a joy for our lives. We choose to have fun and God leads me to the things we need to do to make our time together a blessing to each other. We pray for each other and celebrate each other's accomplishments in life. I am part of the family of God and no one can take that away. I was bought with the blood of Jesus Christ, therefore I belong to Him and no one can separate me from His love. GLORY!"

▪ **Loss of reputation.** Do you get looks or whispers? Have rumors been spread about you on social circles? Have you been shunned at church, school or other places in the community? A loss of reputation hurts.

Sometimes folks are cold in their whispers and their reaction to you when they see you. I remember my daughter; Mary Charlene being shunned at school. It had nothing to do with divorce but jealousy of her accomplishments. This kind of shunning is the same no matter what the situation is. I had taught her and Barjeana every morning out of this little book, Favor the Road to Success by Bob Buess. They both had walked in such favor at their schools that when a temptation came to be pushed away or rejected they both rose above it. The particular situation with Mary Charlene was she was valedictorian. Another person wanted that as well and she was new in the school. So even though they failed a test and cheated on an exam the school allowed them to share the honor. Many of the kids would talk about her as she went around to her classes. I was so proud of her the way she acted. She acted like they did not exist. Her teacher told me that she realized what they were doing but Mary seemed totally oblivious to their talk. She was hidden in a bubble. I believe God can do that for all of us. Keeping our eyes on the Lord has every-thing to do with how you survive anything like this. You can thrive instead of surviving.

Whatever you do, don't become bitter and listen to the devil's lies that say you might as well do what they are saying about you. Live holy and let God redeem your reputation. He knows how valuable your reputation is.

1 Timothy 3:13 BSB
For those who have served well as deacons acquire for themselves a high standing and great confidence in the faith that is in Christ Jesus.

Proverbs 3:4 NLT
Then you will find favor with both God and people, and you will earn a good reputation.

CONFESSION: "My life is hid with Christ in God. My sins are forgiven by the blood of Jesus Christ. Nothing can hinder me from serving God with my whole heart, soul and body. I live a holy life and allow God to restore my reputation. This makes me rejoice seeing by faith His restoration of my reputation. HALLELUJAH!"

▪ **Loss of social status.** Even if your credit is still good, as a single person you may have to pay higher insurance rates, fall in different risk categories, and be assumed "less stable" than married people.

The prejudices of this world system can try to make you angry and even sulk. Remember which system you live in. Your life is in a Kingdom that the world knows not of. You may need to be a fighter to stand up for injustices, but whatever you do, don't become an angry

PITIFUL or POWERFUL

bitter person who demands their way of other people. When suffering an injustice, tell the devil where to go. There are kind ways to take care of this when we know our authority in Christ. Be firm and steady and watch for the favor of God to work on your case. If everyone else has difficulties in this area, the favor of God can change things for you.

Luke 2:52 NIV
And Jesus grew in wisdom and stature, and in favor with God and man.

> **CONFESSION:** "I am just like Jesus. I am full of wisdom and stature. I have favor with God and man. I grow in these things as I move forward in God. No hindrances can or will stop me from flourishing and men shall see it and be glad. GLORY!"

> ▪ **Loss of credibility.** Did you mentor your couples, teach, write, speak or counsel others about marriage?

Many times a person will refuse to get a divorce when they possibly should because they don't want to hurt other people. When it is a case of abuse you have to make uncomfortable decisions to preserve your life and those who love you. Our credibility is so important but no one can know exactly what goes on in a marriage behind closed doors. This loss of helping others in marriage when we could not help ourselves can be a shameful thing to us.

There was a minister acquaintance who had an abusive doctor husband who no one knew what was going on. She had a divorce once before but did not want to hurt the ministry by divorcing again. It was brought to light that he was giving her drugs that altered her mind and she died a very traumatic death. He was not convicted of the murder as it was hard to prove this. She had said enough to friends that before and after she died there was an investigation. He was imprisoned for a season. However, to protect the ministry above her good judgment, she lost her life prematurely. Every one of us who loved her and her ministry would not have placed shame on her. For fear of shame we can make bad decisions.

Romans 10:11 KJV
For the scripture saith, whosoever believeth on Him shall not be ashamed.

Psalms 25:2-3 NIV
2. I trust in you; do not let me be put to shame, nor let my enemies triumph over me.
3. No one who hopes in you will ever be put to shame, but shame will come on those who are treacherous without cause

PITIFUL or POWERFUL

- **Loss of dreams and goals.** Did you plan for a cabin on the lake or a RV to travel in after retirement?

So often grieving over what was to be can be so destructive. There comes a time where you have to let it go. God has good plans for you and you have no idea when you trust in Him just how He will make this crooked place straight for you. I love this Scripture in *Jeremiah 29:11*.

Jeremiah 29:11 AMP
For I know the plans and thoughts that I have for you,' says the Lord, 'plans for peace and well-being and not for disaster to give you a future and a hope.

CONFESSION: "My hope is in God. He alone has my future in His hands. He has ways to lead and provide for me. He gives me new hope, new vision and new goals as I seek His face above all else. Praise God for my new hope and future for it is brighter than I have ever known. I will not grieve the past goals and dreams. God's dreams for me are better than I could ever dream of. He puts His dreams for me in my heart and I have faith for them to come to pass. GLORY TO GOD!"

- **Loss of hope for another marriage.** Younger people seem to assume there is still plenty of time to find another mate. Older people aren't so sure and sometimes feel desperation and despair. Where do you fit in?

The same Scripture I used with *Jeremiah 29:11* really applies to this particular desire too. If you desire to remarry, then talk to the one who knows where the new wife or husband are. If we try to do it on our own, we could make another big mistake. Our hope is in God, not in a good looking person or a dream boat. We are never too old for God to step in. No matter what our age, God can come on the scene for us. I read of people who are in the rest home but they find love and reconnection in marriage. So there is always hope.

Romans 15:13 NIV
May the God of hope fill you with all joy and peace as you trust in him, so that you may overflow with hope by the power of the Holy Spirit.

CONFESSION: "My hope is in God. Victory is mine now. I am not a lost soul looking for a place to abide. I need not be disturbed for my God leads me in paths of righteousness. He can hook me up with a person who has the same vision, same goals and loves me and loves to be loved. I let God work and His

35

will for me be above all my own fleshly desires. I speak to him about choices that I know not of. He knows all things and is willing to bless my life. GLORY!"

▪ **Loss of sleep.** A major contributor to depression after divorce is an inability to sleep through the night. Armies have used sleep deprivation as a form of torture. This loss can compound all your other losses.

Loss of sleep can be serious. It can cause depression. I should say if not taken care of it will cause depression. It will cause you stinking thinking. Only 10 % of the population have chemical imbalances according to Dr. Don Colbert. He makes these statements about sleep. I add it can cause stinking thinking.

Dr. Colbert says, *"We can replace stinking thinking. He states most of our behavior is learned and can therefore be unlearned even if it's rooted in one's genes. Emotions do not die. We bury them but we are burying something that is still alive. Emotions buried alive, never die."*

I add they just keep surfacing during pressure or they show up in manifesting disease in our bodies. Even children can suffer from depression.

There are vitamins that can be taken to help with sleep rather than having a prescription drug that can be habitual and make it more difficult as time goes on. Getting up to pray over situations and casting them before the Lord can help you relax and put you back to sleep.

Certainly anger needs to be settled. It needs to be dealt with. We do not lash out at others without an apology. The Scripture tells us not to allow the sun to go down on our anger. I am giving you four different versions of this Word from the Lord of *Ephesians 4:26*

New International Version
"In your anger do not sin": Do not let the sun go down while you are still angry,

New Living Translation
And "don't sin by letting anger control you." Don't let the sun go down while you are still angry,

English Standard Version
Be angry and do not sin; do not let the sun go down on your anger,

PITIFUL or POWERFUL

Berean Study Bible
"Be angry, yet do not sin." Do not let the sun set upon your anger,

Sleep deprivation is something armies use to get the truth out of their enemies. Let us do everything we know to do to avoid loss of sleep. It can be very dangerous to you, your work, and your well-being.

Getting to the root cause of the lack of sleep is so important. I have dealt with some of the root causes possible concerning lack of sleep.

I remember as a little girl one time my Mom spoke to our pastor while in the hospital about her sleep issue. He gave her a Scripture I have never forgotten. It stuck in my mind to this day. *The Word of God is sharper than a two-edged sword.*

Psalms 3:5 NIV
I lie down and sleep; I wake again, because the LORD sustains me.

> **CONFESSION:** "I lie and sleep for my Lord is with me. I take authority in Jesus Name over all tormenting thoughts that rise up against me. I take authority over every fear and worry. My place is a place of peace. I can lie down and sleep. All deficiencies in this body be filled in Jesus Name. I let anger go and I do not hesitate to apologize to anyone I have displayed my temper to."

> **PRAYER:** "Forgive me Lord, I choose not to allow the sun to go down on my wrath or anger. Give me the integrity to take care of it with others in Jesus Name. AMEN!"

If you have other losses not listed here, write them down and lift them in prayer to the Lord. A suggestion that if you have children, get them to write down the things they miss. It can help open up help for them in dealing with their feelings of loss.

He delights in restoring His children in every area of life. Find Scriptures that speak of restoration. Acknowledge the losses but give them to your heavenly father. He already knows about them, but He still wants you to give Him the list. He wants you to trust that He not only will restore what you have lost, but He will give you even greater blessings than you have ever known.

PITIFUL or POWERFUL

Joel 2:25
And I will restore to you all the years that the locust hath eaten, the cankerworm, and the caterpillar, and the palmerworm, my great army which I sent among you.

Only God can heal the pain you feel. It is good to have a friend who can stand with you, understand your hurt, but not allow you to stay in the hurt forever. They need to be a person of prayer and support. You have taken a huge hit mentally, emotionally, physically, sexually, financially and spiritually. Rushing to make you get over it is not wise. Things won't be the same anymore but God will make them better if you allow Him to. When we are honest about our feelings and fears, He is there for us. He will give us guidance and peace.

Psalms 37:23
The steps of a good man are ordered by the Lord: and he delighteth in his way.

The enemy may lie to you and tell you that you are not a good man or woman after going through a divorce. The good that this Scripture is referring to is our right standing with the Lord Jesus Christ. If you have asked Jesus to be your Savior this Scripture is for you. If you have not done so, and you desire a life of peace, hope, and joy. Pray this prayer.

> **PRAYER:** Dear Heavenly Father, I come to you in the Name of Jesus. You said in your Word, *"Whosoever shall call upon the name of the Lord shall be saved. (Romans 10:13)* I am calling on your name, I repent of every evil deed or thought. Wash me in the blood of Jesus Christ and cleanse me from every sin. You also said, *"If thou shalt confess with thy mouth the Lord Jesus, and shalt believe in thine heart that God hath raised him from the dead, thou shalt be saved. For with the heart man believeth unto righteousness; and with the mouth confession is made unto salvation. (Romans 10:9-10)* I believe in my heart Jesus Christ is the Son of God. I believe that he died and He was raised from the dead for my justification. And I confess Him as my Lord today. I have now become *the righteousness of God in Christ. (2 Corinthians 5:2)* … and I am saved! Thank you Lord!

If you prayed this prayer from your heart and for the first time, begin to fellowship with the Lord by talking to Him. *1 John 1:9* says, *If we confess our sins, He is faithful and just to forgive us our sins, and to cleanse us from all unrighteousness.* Make sure let someone know you prayed this prayer and meant it. Read the Bible. Start in Proverbs in the Old Testament or the book of John in the New Testament.

You may have not been aware of wrong doing previously but once you have invited Christ into your life, you will sense when you have done something wrong. This Scripture from *1 John 1:9* is there for you. Draw on its power and ask for His divine help. We are to strive for a life without sin but when we miss it we can always remember this Scripture and don't let the enemy put a heavy weight on your shoulders saying, "You blew it now." He always tries to make us feel there is no hope for us, we are too bad but God does not see you that way. He paid a big price for you. He is ever ready to bring you back to fellowship with Him.

■■■

3. THE PAIN AND RELIEF OF ACCEPTANCE

Getting to the place of realizing that things are not working out can be a painful place and once accepted you can have a sigh of relief.

To start the climb upward you can help yourself by

- Counting Your Blessings

- List your blessings

- Read your Bible, pray, listen to teaching tapes and listen to praise music.

- You may need to visit your doctor to check on your well-being.

- Start some form or fun exercise, such as walking in a beautiful area. Swimming is another great exercise and it can be refreshing. There are many forms of exercise that are beneficial. Stay away from mystical and new age ways of exercise such as meditations. It depends what you are meditating on. God and His Word is one thing that will make your way prosperous. Some forms of exercise suggest you blank your mind and think on nothing. Be aware that the enemy loves to get in your head and take advantage of a blank mind.

- Rework your budget, so that you're not stressed

- Force yourself to socialize. Start simple like lunch with a friend.

- Rent a funny video.

- Go to a movie even by yourself.

- Buy someone a gift. Depression is very self-focused.

- Move your furniture or clean your closets.

- Learn to get healthy boundaries so you are not a victim.

- Quit keeping secrets. Confidences are different than secrets.

Make a list of things that have tried to make you feel you have lost power over your life.

We need to take time to work out how we got to the place we were, what really happened and what in us needs to be fixed.

Mental and emotional problems never just automatically go away. They are embedded and will constantly cause us problems if we do not deal with them. We must take steps that bring healing.

With God we can get over a divorce and the death of a loved one. The memories will be there but with Jesus the pain can be removed. We can become healed and live a fruitful life.

MOVING AT OUR OWN PACE

When I write about us moving at our own pace, I never want to allow you to aid yourself to stay where you are in pain, defeat or destruction. Setting a time limit to walk through something that has been so painful is not wise. To stay in the self-pity is never wise. Allow your self-time to get through the harm done.

The man at the pool of Bethesda waited thirty-eight years. *[John 5:1-8]*

The woman with the issue of blood had been ill for twelve years. *[Luke 8:43-48]*

What did these two have in common? Write down the commonness.

PITIFUL or POWERFUL

They both had to do something. Healing just did not fall on them.

What steps do you need to take toward your healing?

_____

_____

Don't let this period of time in your life be a waste of time. Let healing come by recognizing all the areas I have suggested previously in this writing.

I believe so many people need healing in this area. They remarry with the same distrust, dismay and heart hurt. Rejection keeps on reaping more rejection unless set free from it. If these things have not been healed your chance for happiness is almost impossible. Large percentages of people who are divorced and remarry have the same problems and divorce again.

Don't look for the right person, be the right person. Focus not on someone helping me.

Concentrate on what you can add to their life by your wholeness.

I know some in the body of Christ who have married many times. When I was in Bible School, young and old alike seemed to have this problem. A few students would go home during the holidays and get married, without regard to the person they were marrying being of similar vision. I know of a case where this happened. A man in his 50's. He was a very striking person. He had funds. He was a leader and divorced previously due to having given his life to Jesus and his wife wanted nothing to do with him. He married during the Thanksgiving Holiday to a lady in his hometown. When he came back to school his wife stayed back in the hometown. She did return with him after Christmas. I saw them several times at different functions. They seemed fine, but I felt something was not quite right. I had visited with his wife several times and really liked her. One day the Lord gave me a word for him. He responded with you don't know how badly I needed that word. I asked someone after missing him at school what was going on with him. They said he had dropped out because his wife was divorcing him. I went to talk to her. I was hoping I could help them both. She had married him out of a physical attraction without knowing the call of God on his life. When they had married he had not told her he was called to be a Pastor. She had been raised Catholic and to be a Pastor was like being a Priest. When he came to realize his calling he came home and told her and she

PITIFUL or POWERFUL

freaked out. She could only relate to Nuns and Priests and felt unworthy to be in such a position. To her this was unobtainable as they were very holy people. She said to me I could never be good enough to be a Pastor's wife. Unfortunately, she divorced him.

A few months later someone gave me his new phone number. I called him as a friend to tell him that I felt the Holy Spirit wanted to continue his schooling. I also told him that he needed to be careful as he was vulnerable emotionally. He seemed to be okay, but he did not really appreciate me saying that to him. I did not know he was already planning to be remarried within a few weeks. I lost contact, but I pray all went well for him and his new life. God is such a restoring God, however; we need to walk carefully with Him.

If you are considering marriage make sure that the person fits into the purpose that God has for your life. If they do not, you must let them go. If you are called to ministry, you should marry someone who is called alongside with you. They don't have to necessarily be in the pulpit but they are called to walk with you in that calling.

The call of God is irrevocable.

> *Romans 11:25*
> *For the gifts of God are without repentance.*

In this verse the word, *gifts* from the Strong's Concordance (# 5486) is a spiritual endowment. It is the same word *charisma*. The word *calling* in Strong's Concordance (#2821) is invitation. The word *repentance* is irrevocable. (#287 in Strong's Concordance).

So the invitation to be used of God is irrevocable.

You should make sure the person you are considering spending the rest of your life with shares the same goals and vision for life that you have.

You do not get divorced because you think you have married the wrong person. If they do not fit into the call of God on your life, you will have to live a life of prayer. It may be hard for you but *1 Peter 3:1* says, *"Likewise, ye wives, be in subjection to your own husbands; if any obey not the word, they also may without the word be won by the conversation of the wives."*

The word 'conversation' means behavior. (Strong's Concordance #391)

PITIFUL or POWERFUL

You do not seek a divorce just because you decided you do not like the person. If they are abusive or committing adultery then you must look at the Word of God that says, you are released.

> *Matthew 19:8 AMP*
> *"I say to you; whosoever dismisses (repudiates, divorces,) his wife, except for unchasity, and marries another commits adultery and he who marries a divorced woman commits adultery."*

This last sentence was added by the translators and is not in the original manuscript. The first part we can be sure Jesus spoke of. The Jews were divorcing just for little reasons like their toast was burned. Jesus spoke and said you only have one reason to divorce. Jesus said if you looked upon a woman to lust, you have already committed adultery in your heart. *[Matthew 5:28]*

_____

_____

_____

_____

A good idea to look this Scripture up and write it out. Now, this applies to ladies too. I have known women who have a serious problem with lust. It is just as serious as with a man. It can lead you to destroy homes. It starts in the flesh but then the enemy can take possession. You must take authority over evil thoughts.

I know of several different situations where a married person is extremely close with a person of the opposite sex. This "we are just close friends stuff," when one or both of you are married is not right. If you are really friends, then both you and your spouse should see the person together or not at all. You should never allow yourself to be in a compromising situation or that may appear to be compromising.

In this day people seem to throw out the Scripture about abstaining from the appearance of evil.

> *1 Thessalonians 5:22 KJV*
> *Abstain from all appearance of evil.*

PITIFUL or POWERFUL

1 Thessalonians 5:22 AMP
Abstain from every form of evil [withdraw and keep away from it].

I add whatever form or whatever kind it may be.

If you are attracted to someone else other than your mate, you need to really get your flesh under through the Word of God and prayer. Attraction can come and go, but commitment is what is important. Your family needs a solid foundation.

■■■■
4. BREAKING THE SOUL TIE

There is not a particular Scripture that uses the words soul tie, but it is certainly a tie of the emotions like no other bond there is on earth. Sometimes we speak of an unhealthy soul tie. That has to do with friends who are always in each other's business, or ties between people of the same sex that interferes with their family life. It can be between people of the opposite sex as well. If a person is completely obsessed with someone and has to see him or her, or else they are really upset, there is a soul tie.

I have an example of an unhealthy soul tie.

In one of my classes I was taking on this subject a young woman had an experience that she shared with us. It is a great example of an unhealthy soul tie. She went back to her hometown to be with her family. While she was there she caught herself being caught up in her mind about contacting a young man that she was involved with before she was married. She denied in her mind that there was any connection. But all she could think of was being together with him.

She had learned in our classes about unhealthy soul ties. She began to pray and she admitted to herself what was going on. She prayed it out by renouncing this soul tie. When she did the thoughts came under the blood of Jesus.

Through someone she found out he was an alcoholic and in jail. But there was such a drawing in her soul area to find him and be with him. She had a wonderful husband and lovely child. Her soul could have led her into such a mess that she would have lost her fam-

PITIFUL or POWERFUL

ily. It would have been her soul (her mind and emotions) leading her and not her spirit. The Spirit of God certainly would not have led her to do such a thing. The Lord may have you pray for such a person, but not make physical connection or contact longing to be with them physically. Protect yourself from harm and alarm with these kind of temptations.

When we live with love, have children with, make love to a person you become one flesh or you have a soul tie or one flesh union with that person. You bond mentally, emotionally, and physically. When the physical relationship is destroyed either by divorce or death, it is like parts of you go with the other person and parts of the other person stay with you. The parts that stay with you are the soul ties we are going to address.

In our society we have funerals for a good-bye at death. If they knew the Lord it is a celebration of their life.

All kinds of good-byes go on in our lives. There are good-bye parties when we leave a job, move or at the end of school. These are all part of healing, closure or breaking a soul tie.

The following suggestion may seem silly or way out, but remember it is only a suggestion.

Some painful memories can be stored in a family member's or your own attic. You know where they are but they are out of sight.

There are several ways to break soul ties. You can take the entire leftover memento; photos, gifts or write down on paper your memories and feelings. Now you can place all of these in a box and wrap them beautifully, dig a deep hole in the ground; you and your prayer warrior partner give them to the Lord as you bury them. When the painful emotions try to resurface, remind yourself that you have given that emotion to the Lord and thank Him for taking care of it for you.

One time we were in a meeting and every time we got together someone would mention the failure of a certain pastor in our lives. I asked the Lord how to handle this, and He said to have the people write the grievances and failures down, light a fire in the fireplace and toss each item into the flames and give it to the Lord. We pledged not to mention it anymore. This set us all free and particularly the people who had to see this person regularly. Share this victory with your prayer partner where you can laugh and cry together but walk through it together in peace.

If there is a list of soul ties that have come to mind during this teaching, list them and let

45

them go. _____

_____

_____

_____

_____

I know of a person who remarried to a man who seemed very loving and kind. However, he left his wife's photo up after he married my friend and refused to put her photo up. He also left her without any support after his death. His children told her she had one day to leave after the death. She was grieving and hurt added to hurt. Ask yourself why am I doing this? Am I so desperate for companionship I will settle for anything not to be alone.

Another person married a man who had a lovely child. She loved the child and was glad to take the child and raise him. It became clear he was only looking for a woman to take care of his child. After marriage he became possessive, not allowing her freedom to be with her friends ever. He never allowed her to attend any church functions or dinners with fellowship. She had a nice job which she had for years. To finally get rid of him she had to pay him to get out of the marriage. Her soul had led her into this bad situation. She was so hungry for someone to be with and she thought he was prince charming and needed her. Today she is back to square one. I pray she is wiser now and will not allow her soul to dictate to her these unhealthy soul ties connections. She had ignored the signs before marriage.

It is vital to pray over every friendship and get ourselves healthy emotionally so God can send us a healthy person emotionally.

■■■■■
5. RELEASE

Only a few times in my life have I heard of people who were divorced from each other getting back together. There has to be a release in order to go on with your life. It is through prayer and making a new life can release come. To continue on causing each other grief and hurt is strife. When we walk in strife, there are all kinds of trouble.

I know of a case where a young couple was divorced. They both went to the same church.

PITIFUL or POWERFUL

The young man left the church, but he desired to come back. The pastor left it up to the former wife. She thought she would not be acting in love to say I would prefer he does not return. So she said, okay with me. Inside it was not okay with her. I saw him harass her after almost every service. So many people could not see it because it was subtle. He would say ugly things in front of the children like, "My goodness a kiss is not necessary they are just coming with me." Other hateful things would come out of his mouth. He was out of order. He evidently was not releasing her to raise the children and he wanted to be their all in all. He did not have the authority to act that way and do damage to their children emotionally. To see this happening broke my heart.

If you are harboring any ill feelings of unforgiveness you must let it go. Ask God to heal you of painful memories you may have. I think by this time of reading this book and workbook surely you have been able to let it go. In case you have not, you must do it.

Bitterness dries the bones.

> *Proverbs 3:5-8*
> *5. Trust in the Lord with all thine heart; and lean not to thine own understanding.*
> *6. In all of thy ways acknowledge Him, and He will direct thy paths.*
> *7. Be not wise in thine own eyes: fear the Lord, and depart from evil.*
> *8. It shall be health to thy navel, and marrow to thy bones.*

■ ■ ■ ■ ■ ■
6. THE WHOLENESS OF SINGLENESS

Dr. Myles Munroe, the author of *'Single, Married, Separated and Life After Divorce'* has a great message for divorced men and women. He teaches that we are to be *"separate, unique and whole."*

Separate: means to set or keep apart, to make ready.

Unique: being the only one of its kind. Being without equal or rival. Unusual.

Whole: Not divided or disjoined, restored, healed, sound, healthy, restored to a whole person again.

PITIFUL or POWERFUL

How does that sound? As a single you are all of those wonderful things. You are distinct, unequaled, and perfect…..like a rare and brilliant gem. Forget that you don't fit- instead, understand you are unique.

- Remember this time in your life is a season and not an eternity.

- If you struggle with loneliness and isolation in your singlehood, God can meet these emotional needs in various ways, not just through a new romantic relationship.

- No one is perfectly content here on earth. God saves that for heaven.

- Use this time to become the most beautiful person you can be, inside and out. Then if God blesses you with someone new, you will be ready!

- Reach out to others.

- Remember you are still healing. Get lots of rest and trust God.

- Thank God every day for the gift of singleness. He will give you wisdom and peace.

If you desire to remarry, you should keep your focus on the Lord. Tell Him what you desire in a mate. Let Him find the mate for you. List the qualities you desire in a mate. Write them down.

_____

_____

_____

_____

_____

_____

_____

_____

If you are female remember *Proverbs 18:22*
   Whoso findeth a wife, findeth a good thing, and obtaineth favor of the Lord.

Call me old fashioned, but notice this Scripture does not say she who finds a husband finds a good thing. Usually she who finds a husband is a mess. If you keep your focus on the Lord, and He is truly first in your life, He will give you the desires of your heart.

This Scripture takes all the pressure off of us. Place the pressure on the Word and live by it.

If and when you start dating, you want to be sure you do it God's way. Here is a **definition of Sex** that works for singles of all ages.

▶ **S - Surrender your will to God's way.** Remember that God did all the work in putting the first couple together. Adam longed for a mate and God took care of everything. God is no respecter of persons. He can and will do it for us. Getting involved in a romantic relationship and becoming sexually active, even if we are in love, is not God's way. This is the world's way. God's way is to learn about ourselves, learn about the other person, get married and then intimacy. Are you willing to trust Him to bring that special someone to you?

▶ **E - Educate yourself.** You can find hundreds of excellent books tapes, videos, and classes to show us how to communicate, honor, respect and love each other the right way. These will include tips on staying chaste, parenting, and anything you want to know about having a successful relationship. What usually holds a person back from educating themselves in relationships is the fear of facing themselves. They are afraid they will have to change or we may find out the person has a few faults. Sometimes just pure laziness is the reason. You may want everything easy like a fairy tale. Well, it is not that way. Fairy tales are wonderful but this is real life.

▶ **X - Cross out what the world says.** Refuse to buy into the world's messages of self-absorption, self-fulfillment, self-satisfaction, and obsession with beauty, sex and seduction. Some people are afraid to say no to the world and yes to God's way. They are afraid life will be boring, deprived, and dull. They seem to forget God and His way offers true joy.

Josh Harris writes in his book, *'I Kissed Dating Goodbye'* that he chose to quit dating all together. He refused to kiss his girlfriend until their wedding day. Now that sounds extreme to most people. He had to make this decision for himself. We all know kissing can open the door to lots of passions that you may not be able to take control of at a certain point. **Self-control is very important.**

It is important when or if you date, that you draw a line where it will keep you from be-

PITIFUL or POWERFUL

coming too intimate, either physically, or emotionally too soon. Current dating styles tell us to enjoy each other while we can, with no regard to the future, because that might cramp our style. Don't push your expectations for commitment on me right now is the world's way. We can talk about that later (maybe). If it works fine. If it doesn't don't blame me. Dating is primarily self-centered and self-protective.

Courtship is all about getting to know each other mentally and emotionally without the false illusion of intimacy that sex introduces. You already know that sex is great, and you can wait because you want more than the thrill of romance. God made both you and your partner to need true intimacy and complete trust, neither one of you want to do anything to damage that. If you cannot trust your future mate with your Chasity before marriage how can you trust them with the opposite sex after marriage?

PART THREE
Dealing with Sickness

■

1. ACCEPTING WHAT GOD HAS DONE FOR ME

The reason I am going to deal with sickness is because it does affect a person in their emotions as well as their body.

In this section of our study you will be expected to do a lot of writing. One of the best ways to learn is to read out loud and then to write what you have read. I want the Word of God on healing to get down into your spirit.

Look up and write *Matthew 8:16-17*

_____
_____
_____
_____
_____
_____
_____
_____

We see from the Scriptures in numerous places that Jesus has borne our sicknesses and our sin. This gives us a foundation to receive our healing.

Many people feel that God is punishing them with sickness. Read *James 1:13-14, 17 and 20*

PITIFUL or POWERFUL

What do these verses say about God?

_____

_____

_____

They all seem to say the same thing. *"God cannot be tempted with evil. Neither tempteth He any man."* Strong's Concordance 3985 **Tempted means discipline, prove, tempt, try.** These are the meanings we can easily understand. So with these definitions we can safely translate this Scripture to say God said in His Word, do not say God is disciplining me with sickness and any other evil. God is trying me and proving me with evil that has or is happening in my life. DON'T SAY IT!

Acts 10:38 Jesus was going about *healing all that were oppressed of the devil.* Now if Jesus was going about healing all who were sick and called it an oppression of the devil then we must recognize this world was cursed through Adam and Eve, but we are delivered from that curse through Jesus Christ.

If God was proving, trying and tempting people with sickness why would Jesus come along and heal them? Think. Don't allow man's traditional teachings to get in your mind.

When we are sick, we are not to say that God is trying me, tempting me, or proving me with sickness. Yet we hear Christians say these things a lot.

What does *James 1:17 and 20* say? Write it and place it before your eyes.

_____

_____

_____

_____

Every good and perfect gift is from above, and cometh down from the Father of lights, in whom there is no variableness, neither shadow of turning.

For the wrath of man worketh not the righteousness of God.

Sickness is not a good and perfect gift, so it could not come from God. Healing has nothing to do with us making ourselves good enough to receive it. God is a loving Father

PITIFUL or POWERFUL

Who wants to do good things for His children. He wants to make us well. Write it for yourself to see *Acts 10:38*.

_____

_____

_____

_____

_____

This Scripture tells who the author of sickness is and it is certainly not God.

In order to get well, we must decide that God wants us well. Read and write *3 John 2*.

_____

_____

_____

_____

Beloved, I wish above all things that thou mayest prosper and be in health, even as they soul prospereth.

God has instructed the New Testament Church to be anointed with oil. If you are not attending a church that believes in doing this then find someone who does believe in it and meet together.

James 5:14-16 NKJV
14. Is anyone among you sick? Let him call for the elders of the church, and let them pray over him, anointing him with oil in the name of the Lord.
15. And the prayer of faith will save the sick, and the Lord will raise him up. And if he has committed sins, he will be forgiven.
16 Confess your trespasses to one another, and pray for one another, that you may be healed.

Sickness can be because we have not forgiven and allowed God to heal us in areas of our soul. No condemnation when I say this, but we must look to see if there is any harboring of ill will.

PITIFUL or POWERFUL

If your child became sick and you made them that way, you would be a terrible parent. How much more, our God is not a terrible God to do that to us or our family? He wants to heal His children and He has the ability to do it.

Look up and read the following Scriptures

John 10:10

_____

_____

_____

_____

John 10:10 NKJV
The thief does not come except to steal, and to kill, and to destroy. I have come that they may have life, and that they may have it more abundantly.

Matthew 4:23-24 KJV

_____

_____

_____

_____

_____

_____

_____

23. And Jesus went about all Galilee, teaching in their synagogues, and preaching the gospel of the kingdom, and healing all manner of sickness and all manner of disease among the people.
24. And his fame went throughout all Syria: and they brought unto him all sick people that were taken with divers diseases and torments, and those which were possessed with devils, and those which were lunatick, and those that had the palsy; and he healed them.

Psalms 103:2-5

PITIFUL or POWERFUL

_____

_____

_____

_____

_____

_____

_____

_____

Psalms 103:2-5 KJV
2 Bless the Lord, O my soul, and forget not all his benefits:
3 Who forgiveth all thine iniquities; who healeth all thy diseases;
4 Who redeemeth thy life from destruction; who crowneth thee with lovingkindness and tender mercies;
5 Who satisfieth thy mouth with good things; so that thy youth is renewed like the eagle's.

Proverbs 4:20-22
Write it so to have it before you.

_____

_____

_____

_____

_____

_____

_____

_____

Proverbs 4:20-22 KJV
20. My son, attend to my words; incline thine ear unto my sayings.
21. Let them not depart from thine eyes; keep them in the midst of thine heart.

PITIFUL or POWERFUL

22. For they are life unto those that find them, and health to all their flesh.

The word translated *health* in verse 22 means "medicine."

The Lord is our physician and the medicine He prescribes is His Word. Because God's Word is healing to those that find them, we need to spend the time in His Word studying all that He has said and promised.

Isaiah 55:11

_____

_____

_____

_____

_____

Isaiah 55:11 KJV

So shall my word be that goeth forth out of my mouth: it shall not return unto me void, but it shall accomplish that which I please, and it shall prosper in the thing whereto I sent it.

In *Matthew 8 and 9* you will find several accounts of Jesus healing people, write them down.

_____

_____

_____

_____

_____

_____

Isaiah 53:4-5

_____

_____

_____

_____

_____

_____

_____

_____

Isaiah 53:4-5 LEB
4. However, he was the one who lifted up our sicknesses, and he carried our pain, yet we ourselves assumed him stricken, struck down by God and afflicted.
5. But he was pierced because of our transgressions, crushed because of our iniquities; the chastisement for our peace was upon him, and by his wounds we were healed.

There are numerous Scriptures about the healing of our bodies and emotions. Search out as many as you can so you can have them before you, and have concrete evidence of what the Bible says and not what someone else says. God bless you as you walk out your restoration and healing.

■■

2. HOW TO RECEIVE YOUR HEALING

We receive our healing just like we do our salvation and anything else from God, by faith. Having faith is really not as hard as some like to make it. You see when we are born again; God gives each of us a measure of faith. *(Romans 12:3)* Each time we read and study the Word of God our faith grows. Write *Romans 12:3*

_____

_____

_____

_____

_____

Romans 12:3 MEV
For I say, through the grace given to me, to everyone among you, not to think of himself more highly than he ought to think, but to think with sound judgment, according to the measure of faith God has distributed to every man.

Remember your healing comes through the Word of God. *Isaiah 44:11* tells us that when we speak God's Word, it will accomplish and prosper in the thing it was sent to do. This is why it is so important that you become familiar with healing Scriptures.

Some people feel they do not have enough faith to receive healing. If you fall in this category all you need to do is start using the faith that you have. You will see God work in your behalf.

Healing is a gift to us. Jesus paid for it in full by the stripes placed on His back. All we have to do is receive it with our faith. Faith or believing is an act of our will. It is a decision that we make based on what we have learned to be true about God. It is leaning on Him with absolute trust and confidence. This trust and confidence is based on our knowledge of how good He is and that He will do what He says in His Word. `

■■■

3. ENTERING HIS REST

After we have made the decision to believe, we then rest, knowing that the Word of God will accomplish and prosper in the thing it was sent to do. Real faith is a rest, not a struggle. It is when we really believe that we enter into the rest of God. *(Hebrews 4:3)*

Hebrews 4:3 NKJV
For we who have believed do enter that rest, as He has said: "So I swore in My wrath, 'They shall not enter My rest,'" although the works were finished from the foundation of the world.

There are times when we receive instant results from our prayers and other times when we must wait and be patient. We are not to try and figure out the "how, when and why." We need to be mindful of our thought life during our time of rest. Some people have a tendency to faint in their minds.

PITIFUL or POWERFUL

Hebrews 12:3
For consider Him who endured such hostility from sinners against Himself, lest you become weary and discouraged in your souls.

Our responsibility is simply to remain in childlike faith, knowing that it is impossible for God to fail. Read and write *Isaiah 40:31*.

_____

_____

_____

_____

_____

Isaiah 40:31 NKJV
But those who wait on the Lord Shall renew their strength; They shall mount up with wings like eagles, They shall run and not be weary, They shall walk and not faint.

We should not let self-pity interfere with our healing. When you have been sick for any period of time the temptation is to get into self-pity. When that happens we begin to talk defeat and discouragement. Some people stay sick because of the attention they receive from it. You must create a desire inside of you, by God's Word, to be well. If I know the Lord and I die, I win either way. It is not the greatest thing to not live out your full life doing what God has placed before you to do. I pray the healing anointing in this writing to reach in and touch you deeply inside and outside. Come fully into His goodness in healing for you. Tell the enemy, ***"I refuse to be sick. Jesus paid the price for me and I am taking my healing."***

PITIFUL or POWERFUL

PART FOUR
Overcoming Financial Loss

■

1. FINANCIAL LOSS

In order to be healed in your finances you need to start tithing. Write *Malachi 3:10-11*

_____

_____

_____

_____

_____

_____

Some will try to tell you that tithing is under the law. No, it was there when Abraham was taken to the land God sent Him. That was before the law was given through Moses.

When unexpected funds come, do you plant seed into the Kingdom of God or do you just put it all on bills? It takes faith to plant it. However, I believe we need just to ask the Lord which way it is to be. Do you want me to plant it or did you send this to pay off a bill? Listen to Him and do what He says. He may tell you by impression or other ways to pay a certain amount on a bill and the rest goes to wherever He says.

Write *Malachi 3:8-9*

_____

_____

_____

_____

_____

_____

_____

Do Not Rob God

Malachi 3:8-11 NKJV
8. "Will a man rob God? Yet you have robbed Me! But you say, 'In what way have we robbed You?' In tithes and offerings.
9. You are cursed with a curse, For you have robbed Me, Even this whole nation.
10. Bring all the tithes into the storehouse, That there may be food in My house, And try Me now in this," Says the Lord of hosts, "If I will not open for you the windows of heaven And pour out for you such blessing That there will not be room enough to receive it.
11. And I will rebuke the devourer for your sakes, So that he will not destroy the fruit of your ground, Nor shall the vine fail to bear fruit for you in the field," Says the Lord of hosts;

Did you know that you are robbing God and bringing a curse on your finances when you do not give out of your heart tithes and offerings? The *tithe* is 10% of your income and *offerings* are anything above the 10% tithe. We get the 10% from *Leviticus 28:32 - The tenth shall be holy unto the Lord.*

Did you let out a big sigh and think or say "I can't afford to pay 10%. I won't have enough to pay my bills." When we honor God with our tithes and offerings, He supernaturally stretches the balance we have left. Now, that does not mean you can be foolish with the money you have left. God will not honor foolishness. He will and does rebuke the devourer for your sake. *(Malachi 3:11)*

I remember when my husband passed I received an amount of money miraculously actually. The way he died insurance does not usually pay. I have been a tither since a child. My Mother taught us children to tithe. We did it joyfully and put our small amount in an envelope every week and took it to the house of God. But once I was on my own, a fear tried to hit me. My daughter was helping me with all the expenses by doing my books. She wrote out my tithe check and balanced the checkbook. But fear and panic tried to take me. After all God had done the enemy whispered, "How are you going to make it past these funds?" I had to take authority over the thoughts and give an offering and conquer that fear. God has blessed me beyond words. It has been many years now and God has not let me down. There have been challenges, but every time God made it possible for the challenge to be overcome. I have depended on God to be my husband. He does a great job. I am a sign and a wonder to many people; my social security check is way too low to live on. We have to have a mentality that God is not running out of money and I have plenty. I refuse to have a government limited or poor mentality. I believe God way above that check. I am thankful for it but I certainly don't go by it. I go by God's economy.

If you lose your job or financial investments, shame tries to come on you. Satan will try to keep you under the bondage of shame and depression. If he can keep you depressed over the loss, he will keep you from getting up and trying to come out of it. This is a great time to stand on the devourer being rebuked for your sake. Say it out loud, and say it until you get great joy welling up inside. You have the promise of God, if you are a tither and cheerful giver, you will recover. It may just be a small bump in the road that you hardly noticed if you keep your eyes on Him as your source.

We must deal with the shame and take the promise of God. We must get a new vision of rising up out of our loss and lack.

I know of a man and his wife in Tulsa, OK who lost everything when the oil crunch came years ago in that area. They were faithful to tithe and keep on tithing even with all the losses. Today they are millionaires. Their home is completely paid for and they own several others. They asked the Holy Spirit to teach them concerning finances. It is religious thinking that says that we should be sick, broke and down and out. Religious thinking says we should have nothing and expect nothing. How are we going to reach the world for God if all of us are broke and defeated? The same thinking that we are suffering for Jesus when we get sick or He is teaching us something through it. That same mentality comes to whisper you are out of God's will being so rich and prosperous. We must let that thinking go. I have heard things told on ministers that I knew were honest and forthright in their affairs and someone thinks all they want is their money. Get rid of that thinking. You are giving to God, so let it go. We are responsible to hear from God and give to what He desires us to. Not everything that comes by us is a God thing to give to. A good guideline is, "Is it fruitful? Are they winning people to the Lord? Do they pray for the sick?"

Give and it shall be given to you pressed down shaken together, running over men shall give unto your bosom. So receive the blessings as they come. Don't say, "Oh no, I can't accept that," unless there are controls to the gift. If that is the case, then certainly you must refuse it. Otherwise receive and be grateful.

PART FIVE

Getting Over My Past

■

1. NOT ALLOWING MY PAST TO AFFECT MY PRESENT OR MY FUTURE

Don't give your future to your past. Don't look back. Let go of regret. Love, forgive.

People seem to get caught up in anger. They are angry, they don't want to be angry, but they are REALLY ANGRY. They just can't seem to get back to the place they were before they fell into that pit.

To get out of that pit you must do what you don't feel like doing.

Psalms 107:20

_____

_____

_____

_____

_____

He sent His word and healed them, And delivered them from their destructions.

Ecclesiastes 7:9

_____

PITIFUL or POWERFUL

_____
_____
_____

Talk to God, be real about how you feel. Tell Him, "God, I am angry, I don't want to stay angry; I don't want to be a fool, I ask for your help.

Many people are in prison just because they became angry and took a life or some other extreme behavior. God will forgive but the anger has been costly to them, their friends and their family.

> *Ecclesiastes 7:9 NKJV*
> *Do not hasten in your spirit to be angry, For anger rests in the bosom of fools.*

Write *James 1:19-20*

_____
_____
_____
_____
_____
_____
_____
_____

Write *Ephesians 4:26*

_____
_____
_____
_____
_____

This Scripture does not mean we can get angry in the morning and stay that way all day and then just before bed make peace. It means to be quick to make peace and forgive. It is cruel to not speak to those around you all day or for several days because you are angry

PITIFUL or POWERFUL

about something they did or said.

I am placing the Scriptures from the previous page here so you can see them again.

James 1:19-20
19. So then, my beloved brethren, let every man be swift to hear, slow to speak, slow to wrath;
20. for the wrath of man does not produce the righteousness of God.

Ephesians 4:26 NKJV
Be angry, and do not sin: do not let the sun go down on your wrath,

1 Timothy 2:8

_____

_____

_____

_____

1 Timothy 2:8 NKJV
I desire therefore that the men pray everywhere, lifting up holy hands, without wrath and doubting.

Proverbs 16:32 NKJV
He who is slow to anger is better than the mighty, And he who rules his spirit than he who takes a city.

James 1:21 says that the Word contains power to save our souls. When we are angry it is our soul that needs saving.

2 Corinthians 3:18 says that when we look into the Word, we are transformed into His image.

You may not feel like looking up these Scriptures, but they will pull you out of the pit of anger. You need to get out your concordance and do a study on forgiveness and love. The Bible has the answer to every problem!

PITIFUL or POWERFUL

The Holy Spirit is our Counselor; ask Him what to do to get out and stay out of the pit of anger.

Isaiah 38:17

_____

_____

_____

_____

_____

Let God love you back from the pit of corruption. Condemnation about being in the pit will not get you out of the pit.

> *Isaiah 38:17 NKJV*
> *Indeed it was for my own peace That I had great bitterness; But You have lovingly delivered my soul from the pit of corruption, For You have cast all my sins behind Your back.*

Read *Ephesians 1:4-5; 2:5; 3:17-18.* Paul wrote letters to these churches about carnal behavior, but he also wrote letters about receiving the unconditional love of God. *(Romans 8:35-39)*

> *Romans 8:31-39 MSG*
> *31-39 So, what do you think? With God on our side like this, how can we lose? If God didn't hesitate to put everything on the line for us, embracing our condition and exposing himself to the worst by sending his own Son, is there anything else he wouldn't gladly and freely do for us? And who would dare tangle with God by messing with one of God's chosen? Who would dare even to point a finger? The One who died for us—who was raised to life for us!—is in the presence of God at this very moment sticking up for us. Do you think anyone is going to be able to drive a wedge between us and Christ's love for us? There is no way! Not trouble, not hard times, not hatred, not hunger, not homelessness, not bullying threats, not backstabbing, not even the worst sins listed in Scripture:*
>
> *They kill us in cold blood because they hate you. We're sitting ducks; they pick us off one by one.*
>
> *None of this fazes us because Jesus loves us. I'm absolutely convinced that nothing—*

PITIFUL or POWERFUL

nothing living or dead, angelic or demonic, today or tomorrow, high or low, think-able or unthinkable—absolutely nothing can get between us and God's love because of the way that Jesus our Master has embraced us.

Your victory depends on you receiving the love of God. Write *1 John 4:16-18.*

_____

_____

_____

_____

_____

_____

_____

_____

_____

_____

1 John 4:16-18 NKJV
16. And we have known and believed the love that God has for us. God is love, and he who abides in love abides in God, and God in him.
17. Love has been perfected among us in this: that we may have boldness in the day of judgment; because as He is, so are we in this world.
18. There is no fear in love; but perfect love casts out fear, because fear involves tor-ment. But he who fears has not been made perfect in love.

We either receive the unconditional perfect love of God, or we fear that He is not pleased with us now because we have fallen into a pit.

This is truly our choice of remaining pitiful or powerful.

Read *Matthew 12:11-12; 18:12.* See how God responds when one of His sheep falls into a pit or gets lost.

Be honest with God about how you feel, pour out your complaint before him; but also realize that you are in a sin and truly repent. To repent means to turn away from sin. The help of the Holy Spirit is there for you.

PITIFUL or POWERFUL

We need to identify the root of our anger. Recently something happened in my family that made me very angry. I asked the Holy Spirit, why am I so angry? He identified the source for me. When I realized what I was angry about then I could deal with it. What He told me was not the obvious reason.

Read *Psalms 54*

Read *Psalms 142*

Talk to yourself. Honestly assess the situation and tell yourself the truth. Don't blame everything on other people, circumstances or even the devil. Take responsibility for your actions. Be truthful with other people – don't act like everything is fine when you would really like them to pray with or for you. *James 5:16a AMPC says, Confess to one another therefore your faults (your slips, your false steps, your offenses, your sins) and pray [also] for one another, that you may be healed and restored [to a spiritual tone of mind and heart]...*

Sing or listen to good anointed music – it runs off evil spirits. *1 Samuel 16:14-23* tells how David would play anointed music, and evil spirits would depart from Saul. *2 Chronicles 20:21-22* tells us when the singers began to sing and praise the Lord, He caused confusion among the enemy; and they were self-slaughtered. *Psalms 40:1-3 – He lifted me out of the pit and put a new song in my mouth.* It is impossible to worship God from your heart and stay angry.

Remember, you must do what you don't feel like doing to get out of the pit.

Be willing to die to self. Read *1 Peter 4:1-2. Those who are willing to suffer in the flesh can no longer live in intentional sin.*

The suffering in the flesh occurs when we do what is right without feelings to support us.

1. Apologize to those who hurt us when they should be apologizing themselves.

2. Give away something we desperately want to keep.

3. Be good to others while we are hurting ourselves.

4. Sing praises unto God when we feel like crying.

5. Treat someone good who has mistreated you.

SATAN CANNOT KEEP THIS KIND OF PERSON IN A PIT!

■■

2. FEAR

Fear has to be dealt with. What are you afraid of? We all are challenged at some point with fear. Fear of failure, fear of rejection, fear of people, fear of danger and other fears. They all try to paralyze us.

I have had to overcome fear. I used to be so afraid. Every place we lived in California someone would try to break in on me when my husband was away. Sometimes it happened when he was there. We placed a big tin tub right by the fence so when the person coming into our yard would jump over the fence we would hear it and call for help. It happened so often I got to where I would call friends to come over. They would come over with ball bats, and other things to hit the prowler with. Finally, we moved from that place. It was in the newspaper that this individual who had done this had broken into a house behind where we lived and raped a young lady. The fear drew the same kind of thing everywhere we lived. I got prayer and deliverance over the fear plus I began to quote *Psalms 91* that *He gives His angels charge over me to guard me and keep me in all my ways.* I gained victory over it and it has never happened again. At this time in my life God has given me the promise that I am in a place of safety. I plead the blood of Jesus over my home and sleep like a baby. Fear has to be spoken to and told to leave in Jesus Name. You can and must do it yourself.

I used to have nightmares. They were horrible. They were so real; I could feel the presence of the person in the room in my dream. I would wake up and cover my head with the covers like I was hiding. It was terrifying. I had hands laid on me and anointed with oil and the Pastor rebuked these dreams and I have never had them again. These things are spiritual and need to be handled spiritually.

Write down your fears and place a Scripture beside them that covers and expels them.

_____

_____

PITIFUL or POWERFUL

_____

_____

_____

The things we fear will come upon us. Job said, *"The thing I feared came upon me."* We can have a respect and not challenge certain things but not fear. You don't do something when you are checked by the Lord or warned not to. But you don't have to be afraid to do anything.

To show how far from fear I have come, my son-in-law asked me to go on a zip line. I immediately said, "Yes." This was not your ordinary zip line. It sent you out over a lake backwards up to a high hill. Then it brought you back very fast (someone said fifty-five miles an hour). No fear was on me. I had such peace. I had no cautions not to do it so I did it. I have committed to praying in tongues at least half an hour a day. Most of the time I do more than that. Living a life of prayer has taken care of things that I normally would be afraid to do. I had such a peace and I laughed when the line stopped, and I said, "Wow, that was wonderful." I give God the glory!

Read *1 John 4:16-19*

Perfect love casts out fear. Some of us try to put faith in God, and yet we have no faith in His love for us. Receiving God's love is the first step toward seeing it brought to completion in our lives.

Write *1 John 4:19*

_____

_____

_____

_____

1 John 4:19 NKJV
We love Him because He first loved us.

Perfect love casts out fear because we know that if He loves us, He will surely take care of us. If we love other people with the God kind of love, it opens a door for them to love Him. Love brings peace and fear brings torment. Worrying about the future brings torment.

PITIFUL or POWERFUL

Read *Ephesians 2:10; Jeremiah 29:11.*

God has a plan for your future.

You may be thinking, yes, I know that, "but" or "what if"? No buts, no ifs, JUST BELIEVE!

Read *John 11:40.* Only believe and you will see the glory of God.

STOP TRYING TO FIGURE OUT WHY GOD WOULD LOVE YOU AND JUST BE-LIEVE IN HIS LOVE.

Read *Hebrews 13:5-6.* God promises to meet our needs; therefore, we do not have to fear.

■ ■ ■

3. INSECURITY

Being insecure in who we are and who God says we are will cause us difficulty unless we accept who He says we are. If people intimidate us, they will know it and will take advantage of the way we feel and act. God wants us secure in Him. This takes spending time in God's presence and allowing Him to heal us.

Read *Job 11:16-18*

_____

_____

_____

_____

Job 11:16-18 NKJV
16. Because you would forget your misery, And remember it as waters that have passed away,
17. And your life would be brighter than noonday. Though you were dark, you would be like the morning.
18. And you would be secure, because there is hope; Yes, you would dig around you, and take your rest in safety.

PITIFUL or POWERFUL

Write *Isaiah 54:17*

_____

_____

_____

_____

_____

Isaiah 54:17 NKJV
No weapon formed against you shall prosper, And every tongue which rises against you in judgment You shall condemn. This is the heritage of the servants of the Lord, And their righteousness is from Me," Says the Lord.

This peace, righteousness, security and triumph over opposition are your inheritance. This promise is "No weapon, none, formed against you shall prosper."

Read *Psalm 112:5-9*

Psalms 112:5-9 NKJV
5. A good man deals graciously and lends; He will guide his affairs with discretion.
6. Surely he will never be shaken; The righteous will be in everlasting remembrance.
7. He will not be afraid of evil tidings; His heart is steadfast, trusting in the Lord.
8. His heart is established; He will not be afraid, Until he sees his desire upon his enemies.
9. He has dispersed abroad, He has given to the poor; His righteousness endures forever; His horn will be exalted with honor.

In the above Scripture, we see a man who has dealt generously with the poor, and during his trial he was not afraid. He won. He surely has received the love of God for himself; otherwise he would have had no desire to help anyone else.

Write *1 Peter 3:13*

_____

_____

_____

_____

PITIFUL or POWERFUL

And who is he who will harm you if you become followers of what is good?

Who can harm you if are a zealous follower of that which is good? If a person is loving God, loving others, and doing the best he knows for where he is in his spiritual growth, **there is nothing to fear.**

Insecurity is now at epidemic proportions. It causes great problems in all kinds of relationships. It pressures marriages and friendships. It makes it very difficult for employers to deal with employees. It makes people touchy; they imagine things that are not true. They cannot go forward in life. They stay focused on themselves and are usually hurt if others don't focus on them and their needs. They need outward confirmation continually because they are getting none from within their own heart.

The only cure for this widespread problem is the love of God. Everyone wants to be loved unconditionally – loved for what they are, not for what they do or don't do. God is ready to give us that love if we will humble ourselves and receive it. Read *Isaiah 55:1* – Come and drink freely of the river of life, simply for the self-surrender that accepts the blessing.

■ ■ ■ ■

4. ALLOWING GOD TO HEAL MY MIND AND EMOTIONS

In order for us to receive our healing in our emotions and our mind we must receive God's love. You may ask why does God love me, if He loves me at all? The answer is simple – He just can't help Himself. See *Ephesians 1:4-5* below. We can never be what He wants us to be if He does not love us. BUT HE DOES!

Ephesians 1:4-5
4. For he chose us in him before the creation of the world to be holy and blameless in his sight. In love
5. he predestined us for adoption to sonship through Jesus Christ, in accordance with his pleasure and will—
6. to the praise of his glorious grace, which he has freely given us in the One he loves.

In the entire world God's love is the best medicine for the wounded soul. It is actually the only medicine that can heal the broken hearted and wounded. *Isaiah 38:17 "You have loved my life back from the pit of corruption and cast all my sins behind your back."*

Deuteronomy 7:8

Deuteronomy 7:8 NKJV
but because the Lord loves you, and because He would keep the oath which He swore to your fathers, the Lord has brought you out with a mighty hand, and redeemed you from the house of bondage, from the hand of Pharaoh king of Egypt.

Because God loves us and keeps His oath sworn to our fathers, He brings us out of bondage with a strong arm. GOD DOES IT FOR US; NOT BECAUSE OF US; BUT BECAUSE OF HIS LOVE AND MERCY FOR US. Receive and learn to give to others what He gives to us.

Jeremiah 31:3

Jeremiah 31:3 NKJV
The Lord has appeared of old to me, saying: "Yes, I have loved you with an everlasting love; Therefore with lovingkindness I have drawn you."

This is love with no end, no limits, and no understandable reason for it. God's love is available, free of charge, but it is up to each individual as to whether or not they receive it.

1 John 3:1 NKJV
Behold what manner of love the Father has bestowed on us, that we should be called children of God! Therefore the world does not know us, because it did not know Him.

PITIFUL or POWERFUL

Read *Ephesians 2:4.* God loves us and shows us mercy in order to satisfy the intense love with which He loves us.

Paul stresses the importance of personal revelation concerning God's love.

Ephesians 3:17-20

Be rooted in His love, come to know it in a practical way. Experience if for yourselves. Trees that are well rooted don't blow over easily in the storm. Too many Christians are blown over (they give up or become offended) in the storms of life.

Romans 8:35-39 Don't allow yourself to be separated from God's love. It will help you conquer every problem in your life. When you have trials, don't get separated from God's love. Continually affirm to yourself, "GOD LOVES ME."

(Ephesians 2:3-5)

When you make mistakes, fail God's expectations, or sin continually, affirm to yourself, "God still loves me, He loved me when I was still a sinner, how much more now that I am His own child!"

Romans 5:8-9. While we were yet sinners, He loved us - how much more now.

Look up the following Scriptures about your heart.

Psalms 119:36

_____

_____

_____

Luke 12:24

_____

_____

_____

Acts 5:3

PITIFUL or POWERFUL

_____

_____

_____

James 1:26

_____

_____

_____

I Peter 3:4

_____

_____

_____

l John 3:20

_____

_____

_____

The seat of our emotions is the soul. In my soul is the house for my mind, will and emotions. My mind has thinking abilities. My will has deciding abilities. My emotions have feeling abilities.

We should not deny any of these to operate correctly in our lives. God has given us the ability to think. He has given us the ability to decide. He has given us the ability to feel. It is only when we allow all these to rule us above God's Word that we get in trouble.

When the heart is at peace or filled with love, it communicates harmony to the entire body.

PART SIX
Dysfunction

■

1. WHAT IS DYSFUNCTION?

Webster's says *dysfunction* is impaired or disordered functioning of a bodily system or hereditary qualities.

Anything can be dysfunctional. It can be family, a person, church or governments. This is by no means the final list. Our society as a whole does not even know today what a functional family is. When we say a family is functional, it is supportive, loving, and faces the truth. They do not have hidden secrets that jeopardize each other's well being. When someone in the family faces crisis, they do not leave that person to face it alone. They also face the truth and do not allow wrongs that are committed to be hidden. They are brought into the open and dealt with in love or tough love. They are even helped to overcome.

Dependency and *co-dependency* **are words that we hear a lot. I used to resent hearing the word dysfunctional or dependency. I did not know what they meant so I felt uneasy. When my husband took his life the Holy Spirit brought understanding to me concerning these things. I knew something was wrong. I had cried out to God, I tried to cover these things by being a peacemaker. A peacemaker is very important; however, my peacemaking was misplaced.**

Adam and Eve's family certainly became dysfunctional. Since we are redeemed from the curse of the law and all that goes with the curse, we can be free from this dysfunction.

PITIFUL or POWERFUL

If someone has been accused in your family of wrong doing and they actually did it, but you deny or cover for them, that is dysfunction. Many times it is false accusations and we must stand together. But if it is true we can become paranoid that people are just talking about us or the family member. We become an aid to dysfunction to cover the wrong and it not be dealt with. To always be thinking it is someone else's fault within a family or group makes a dysfunctional atmosphere.

A person should keep very few secrets. Confidences and secrets are two different things. It is an honor to be trusted with a confidence. But to keep a harmful secret inside can be very damaging. Unthinkable childhood trauma such as incest, sexual abuse, can mar the soul. Bitterness and hatred can smolder for decades erupting many years later in the form of terrible nightmares, uncontrollable crying and inability to function in the routines of life. The abuser has told the victim, many times, "Let's keep this our little secret."

They may even tell the victim if you tell it I will know it and I will do thus and so. Living with a horrendous secret only works for so long before the weight of emotional baggage overcomes the hardiest of souls.

Dependency **is a word that means being addicted to people, places or things. A dependant person is one who has to be with certain people and if that person cannot be with them, they fall apart. This can be a family, friendship, etc... This can be one of the reasons for cliques in the Church.** I have seen people set and wait on someone to call and be so obsessed with waiting for their call that they could not function at all until they heard from the person.

There are certain places some people have to be. They are obsessed with that place and they cannot be happy anywhere else. Gambling can become an addiction or dependency. The gambler is obsessed with winning. They have to be where the action is.

Things can be an addiction. It can be food, clothing, or any material thing in life. Addictions make a person not consider anyone else at all, not even what it is doing to them. Nothing should cause us to be oppressed if we do not get it.

Co-dependency is when someone else's problem controls your behavior and life decisions.

► **1.** A co-dependant is a person who is involved in a relationship with someone who

80

is dependent on some kind of abnormal behavior.

▶ **2.** The co-dependent person does not really live his or her own life. They are controlled by the problem of the dependent person.

▶ **3.** They spend most of their time trying to please the dependent person and trying to fix, rescue or help them.

Co-dependency

As long as someone else controls your happiness you are co-dependent. It they are upset you are upset. If they can steal my joy, then I am co-dependent. If their moods affect my moods that is another bad sign.

To break this dependency you must declare your independence and become dependent on God. We are often too involved in other people's problems.

Hebrews 12:1 teaches us to strip off and throw aside every encumbrance, weight, sin and all that clings to and entangles us. Some people become weights – they cling to us and drag us down. If we get entangled in their problems, it will prevent us from reaching our own goals. <u>For example</u>: You may have a goal on Monday morning to spend the day getting your house clean, doing the grocery shopping and laundry. Your needy friend calls, can they come over? She is depressed and needs you to talk to her. Your first thought is "not again." But then you're attacked with guilt, after all you are a Christian. You should be willing to lay aside your desires and help others. But this pattern is repeated over and over with the other person.

If the same person needs so much from us that we cannot obey God, we are out of balance if we keep trying to give in to them.

1. *1 Thessalonians 2:4.* We seek to please God and not man.

2. *Galatians 1:10.* Now am I trying to win the favor of men, or of God? Do I seek to please men?

3. We must all ask ourselves this all-important question, who are we seeking to please?

PITIFUL or POWERFUL

People like this need to learn to go to God. If we keep standing between God and them, we are not ministering, we are hindering.

Types of dependencies that can make you a co-dependent person:

1. Alcohol, drugs, or other substance abuse, denial

2. Controller or manipulator - Those who allow themselves to be controlled are just as wrong as the person controlling. Always remember, "We don't help people if we don't confront them."

1 Corinthians 9:19 AMPC
"For although I am free in every way from anyone's control, I have made myself a bondservant to everyone, so that I might gain the more [for Christ]."

If we refuse to be anyone's slave, we are then free to be his or her servant.

3. Perfectionist - They can make life narrow and miserable for everyone they are in a relationship with. It is almost impossible to please them. His or her perfect plan begins to control everyone's life. Deeply insecure and searching for worth through perfect lives, looks, behavior, and surroundings. When people feel messy inside, extremely neat surroundings somehow make them feel more together. Of course, we should be orderly, neat, and clean; but not extreme and excessive.

4. Workaholic - They always want everybody to work. If anybody is resting or enjoying something they are encouraged to always be working. They are often running or hiding from something painful in their lives. Working all the time prevents them from dealing with the pain of it.

1 Peter 5:8
Be well balanced, for your adversary, the devil roams about like a roaring lion, in hunger, seeking someone to devour.

5. Sexual perversions - Some people cannot perform sexually without perverted behavior. If they are dependent on perversion and insist that you join them, they have made you co-dependent.

6. Hypochondriac - Some control others through their abundance of aches, pains, sicknesses and diseases. It is a never-ending cycle. All they want to talk about is how they feel. Even when a person is genuinely sick, it does no good to constantly think and talk about it. It is difficult to suffer alone, but we must remember that Jesus went to the garden alone, all of his friends fell asleep. There are times in our life when no one can help us but God.

7. Eating disorders - Families can get almost totally destroyed by a member with an eating disorder. (I say not our families as we are learning about the forces of darkness and have power over them). They have to get support from outside their family. I prayed for a young woman in Norway who had a bad disorder. She must have weighed 60 pounds or so. I was asked to come to the home and spend some time with her praying for her. I went and the spirit that was holding her had to let go. The testimony was from that day on she started gaining weight. Later she got better and attended the meeting on a cot. Her Mom came down after the service and told me her daughter was up in the balcony. She was so weak she could hardly do anything. The enemy tried to kill her right there in front of me while telling that spirit to leave. She did her best to jump out of the second floor through a glass window. The spirit holding her was taken authority over and she calmed down. I heard from the Mom later she had gained many kilos. God saved her life.

If a person has *anorexia*, they do not see themselves as skinny. No matter how skinny they get, they still see themselves as fat. This lying devil makes me so angry in the spirit that I must tackle it in His Name. The demonic force will take their life if they don't get delivered.

They must be ready to be helped. In this case, this young woman was not in good condition at all. Her acceptance to come to the meeting was her plea for help.

8. Identity crises problems - Some people are insecure to the point of being sick. They need others to keep them propped up and fixed all the time.

They are touchy about everything. They cannot put much into a relationship. They are too needy. They need, need, need and need. They need to be encouraged, people to understand them, more attention. They need you not to confront them; it is too difficult for them. If you don't invite them everywhere you go, you are rejecting them and on and on.

PITIFUL or POWERFUL

We cannot blame everything on our past to the point of taking no responsibility for ungodly behavior. The key to freedom is if you really want to get well. Read *1 John 5:1-9*

Read *Deuteronomy 7:1-25* - Destroy your enemies and show them no mercy. Don't flirt with your hang ups.

Read *Deuteronomy 7:22* - God will deliver you little by little if you will keep pressing on.

This is your time to break free! Make a decision and refuse to go back to Egypt!

We do not labor in our flesh. God does tell us things like your blessing is here, go there, do this and this will happen.

1. *Matthew 17:27* - The disciples had to go fishing to find money for taxes due.

2. *Mark 3:5* - The man with the withered hand was told to stretch out his hand.

3. *Luke 5:4* - The disciples were told to come out into the deep and get ready for a haul.

4. *Luke 5:24* - The crippled man was told to pick up his bed and walk.

5. *Luke 17:14* - The lepers were told to go show themselves to the priests. And as they went, they were cured and made clean.

6. *John 2:7-8* - Wine for the wedding required the filling of six water pots with water and a command to draw some out and take it to the manager of the wedding feast.

7. *John 9:7* - The blind man after submitting to having saliva and dirt rubbed on him was told to go wash in a pool of water.

8. *John 11:39* - The raising of Lazarus from the dead required the people to take away the stone. Martha's first thoughts and comments were about the stink. Some people never get raised out of their problems, they get caught up in the stink. You would think they would be rejoicing. Jesus was raising a man from the dead and never mind the stink.

9. The enabler - We can actually enable people to stay in bondage by continuing to try to fix them instead of staying balanced and being led by the Holy Spirit.

You may be thinking right now, I don't want to face this, is there any other way? The answer is NO! Problems never just go away unless they are dealt with. If the person you are having problems with right now died or moved to another town, there would always be another person to torment you.

I believe that God is opening prison doors for you; are you willing to walk out? Remember Jesus said, *"I will never leave you, nor forsake you."* He will be with you every step of the journey to wholeness.

PITIFUL or POWERFUL

PART SEVEN
Getting a New Mental Perception

Read *Judges 6:12, 13 and 15*. God saw Gideon differently than he saw himself. Gideon saw himself afraid of the enemy. He saw himself as poor. He was not just poor, but the poorest of the poor. No one in his family had ever done anything great. In studying his family history, there was not one who had accomplished anything worthy of mention. Yet God called Gideon. God told him he was going to save Israel. He had to get a new mental perception through obeying God. This does not come because you came into a prayer line. This comes because you choose to get closer to God. This comes because you choose to obey the impressions of the Holy Spirit in little things. This is a daily thing that needs to be worked on. As an act of our will, we can decide to move out of the depressed state and move into God's plan.

When Gideon obeyed God we see he won so many victories that totally changed his outlook on life. Read *Judges 8:18-22*. This shows a man who saw himself as a king. When he had won these victories for Israel, he became powerful. He asked Zehab and Zalmunna whom they had slain. He asked what they looked like. They answered, "The men we slew looked like the children of a king." Gideon answered, "Those were my brethren, the sons of my mother, if you had saved them alive, I would not slay you. But since you took their lives, and they were who they were, I will have to slay you." Gideon knew who he was. They offered him to be king over Israel, but he refused the position. He said, The Lord shall rule over you, not me or my sons. **He went from being pitiful to being powerful.**

● **Ruth** was a woman whose husband had died. She went with Naomi into a foreign country. She went there knowing no one but her mother-in-law. She had no right in this new land. She was at the mercy of God. She had seen Naomi's God work for her. She said, *"Whether thou goest, I will go."* God raised her up. He gave her a husband who

PITIFUL or POWERFUL

brought her out of poverty. He redeemed her by using Naomi's nearest kinsman. She is mentioned in the linage of Jesus Christ. She got a new mental perception of who she was. It happened in manifestation for her life.

● **Job** was sick. He had lost his whole family. He had lost his cattle. He had lost everything. He held onto God in the midst of it all, and God gave him twice as much as he had before. He prayed for his friends who spoke wrong and unkind things. *Job 42:10*

So many times when people go through things they began to claim they are like Job. They think God is trying them. They can imagine all the horrible things coming to them. First of all, fear was the basis of Job's challenge. He sacrificed for his children over and over in case something went wrong. So worry is not a good thing as we know. Evidently they were party goers and he was not assured they were living right. It seems it was months not years that Job suffered. Scripture shows that this suffering did not go on forever. One thing we have to remember Job did not have authority over Satan as you and I do since Jesus had not died yet and rose again. Jesus gave us power over the devil in His Name. We have to use it. The old saying "Use it or lose it."

Job 7:3 KJV
So am I made to possess months of vanity, and wearisome nights are appointed to me.

Job 7:3 GW
I have been given months that are of no use, and I have inherited nights filled with misery.

According to some Jewish tradition it may have been a year. Others say it was 9 months.

No matter how long it was, one thing; Job did not blame God. There is an expiration date to all trials of life. Keep out the fear and claim God's promises as you walk through life.

Job may not have understood it, but he never blamed God once.

Job 1:22 MSG
Not once through all this did Job sin; not once did he blame God.

This is where we can be an overcomer; by watching the words of our mouth. Never blame

PITIFUL or POWERFUL

God for sorrow you may have been confronted with. If you want to move forward you must not blame God. Satan is our enemy and he wants you to blame God. Don't do it. If you have already spoken against the Lord, ask for forgiveness and don't do it again. Say, "I lean not to my own understanding but God is my helper in time of trouble."

Another thing that Job did was say the thing I feared the most has come upon me. The following writing from the Message Bible shows us very clearly how fear can bring certain happenings that are unpleasant into our life.

Job 3:25 KJV
For the thing which I greatly feared is come upon me, and that which I was afraid of is come unto me.

Job 3:25 MSG
"Instead of bread I get groans for my supper, then leave the table and vomit my anguish. The worst of my fears has come true, what I've dreaded most has happened.

The following Scripture from *Job 1* in the Message Bible tells how worried Job was over his children. We can pray worry prayers and never get off the ground so to speak spiritually. Fear is always an open door to do damage in our lives. *God has not given us a spirit of fear, but of power, love and a sound mind.*

2 Timothy 1:7 KJV
For God hath not given us the spirit of fear; but of power, and of love, and of a sound mind.

Job 1:1-3 MSG
Job was a man who lived in Uz. He was honest inside and out, a man of his word, who was totally devoted to God and hated evil with a passion. He had seven sons and three daughters. He was also very wealthy—seven thousand head of sheep, three thousand camels, five hundred teams of oxen, five hundred donkeys, and a huge staff of servants—the most influential man in all the East!

Job 1:4-5 MSG
His sons used to take turns hosting parties in their homes, always inviting their three sisters to join them in their merrymaking. When the parties were over, Job

PITIFUL or POWERFUL

would get up early in the morning and sacrifice a burnt offering for each of his children, thinking, "Maybe one of them sinned by defying God inwardly." Job made a habit of this sacrificial atonement, just in case they'd sinned.

One of the wonderful things that made the book of Job so interesting that so many people overlook is he had restored to him twice as much as he had before. The key was interceding for his friends who had not spoken good things to him during this trial he went through. We must get to the place we can pray for those who have done or said unkind things. It is part of our restoration.

Matthew 5:44 KJV
But I say unto you, Love your enemies, bless them that curse you, do good to them that hate you, and pray for them which despitefully use you, and persecute you;

Job 42:10-11 MSG
After Job had interceded for his friends; GOD restored his fortune—and then doubled it! All his brothers and sisters and friends came to his house and celebrated. They told him how sorry they were, and consoled him for all the trouble GOD had brought him. Each of them brought generous housewarming gifts.

So Job in the end was powerful and not pitiful. God has power for you. He does not want you pitiful and sad. Take it now in the Name of Jesus. Let Him touch the root of bitterness if there is any. Let it go! You are not designed to carry it.

● **Joseph** had been beaten. He had such a dysfunctional family. This could be a whole seminar in itself. He had brothers who were actually his stepbrothers who hated him. They sold him into slavery. He went into a land where he knew no one. They did not even serve his God. He went to prison for something he did not do. God still brought him out and he became the second in command in Egypt.

When we let God deal with issues in our lives, He sets us free emotionally, and we become powerful instead of being pitiful. Do I want to fulfill the purpose God has for me and become powerful instead of being pitiful? In our soul we have the will which is given to us by God to make decisions. It is our decision. God has already decided He wants us to be powerful.

PITIFUL or POWERFUL

The following are some Scriptures you can pray that will strengthen your inner man and help you become more powerful:

- *Ephesians 3:16* - Strengthen me in the inner man.

- *Ephesians 3:17* - That I may be rooted deep in love and founded securely on love.

- *Ephesians 3:18* - Let me grasp God's love, the breath, length, depth and height of it.

- *Ephesians 3:19* - That I might become a body wholly filled and flooded with God Himself.

- *Philippians 3:10* - That I may "know" Him and the power of His resurrection.

- *Ephesians 1:17* - That He might grant me a spirit of wisdom and revelation.

- *Ephesians 1:18* - That the eyes of my heart be flooded with light.

- *Ephesians 1:19* - That I might know the greatness of His power in me.

- *Philippians 1:10* - That I may learn to sense what is vital and of real value.

- *Philippians 1:11* - That I may be about and be filled with the fruits of righteousness.

- *John 17:12* - That He will keep and protect me from the evil one. (Jesus' prayer)

- *Colossians 1:9* - That I may know God's will.

- *Colossians 1:11-12* - That I may be strengthened with all power, [to exercise] every kind of endurance and patience with Joy, giving thanks.

Salvation

● ● ● ●

If you have never asked Jesus Christ into your life, take the time to submit to God by accepting His Son Who He gave to die for you. He raised Him from the dead that you might have eternal life.

> *Romans 10:9-10 NIV*
> *If you declare with your mouth, "Jesus is Lord," and believe in your heart that God raised him from the dead, you will be saved. For it is with your heart that you believe and are justified, and it is with your mouth that you profess your faith and are saved.*

Religion has made it hard, but the Bible makes it simple. You cannot become good on your own and say, *"I will come to God then."* It will never happen.

Coming to Him just as you are and allowing Him to transform your life, is the way to enter this new life.

> PRAYER:
> *"Father, I come to you accepting the plan You made for my life. I invite Your Son into my heart and accept the forgiveness He paid for on the cross for me. Wash me clean by the Blood of Jesus Christ. I believe Jesus lived and died to pay for my sin on the cross. Then He rose again that I might live in victory. I declare with my mouth, "Jesus is Lord and I believe in my heart that God raised Him from the dead." I proclaim I am a new creation, I am born again. AMEN!"*

If you don't have a Bible, purchase one as quickly as possible. Some wonderful translations are the King James, New King James, Living Bible, Passion and Amplified. Begin by reading the book of John in the New Testament and Proverbs from the Old Testament.

Ask the Lord to lead you to the house of God where they teach about being born again and being filled with the Spirit of God. You might call churches and ask if they believe in being born again and filled with the Spirit. God can lead you to people who are around you already who believe these truths as well.

NOTES

The following references were used:

Backus, William and Chapian, Marie, Telling Yourself the Truth. Minneapolis: (Bethany House Publishers 1989)

Caine, Lynn Widow (New York: Bantam Books 1981)

Ganz, Dr. Richard, The Secret of Self Control (Wheaton Crossway Books 1998)

Harris, Joshua, I Kissed Dating Goodbye (Oregon: Waterbrook Books 1997)

Meyer, Joyce Be Healed in Jesus' Name (Tulsa: Harrison House 2000)

Rachel V. Jeffries is the author of a published book in numerous languages called, **CAPTURE A CITY THROUGH PRAISE,** Intercessory Praise. Available on *www.amazon.com* or through the ministry website *www.rjim.org* Her book is also available on Kindle at amazon.

UPCOMING BOOK TITLES
Victim or Victor, Miracle in Your House, Numerous Ways to Pray, Fasting and Prayer, Dear Joseph subtitled A Personal Letter to Joseph.

She is a songwriter as well as a recording artist. Her CDs **AMAZING LOVE** A 2 CD PACKAGE AND **ATMOSPHERE OF PRAYER AND WORSHIP** are available on ITUNES and SPOTIFY as well as the ministry website *www.rjim.org*

Capture
A City
Through
Praise

Rachel V. Jeffries

www.ingramcontent.com/pod-product-compliance
Lightning Source LLC
LaVergne TN
LVHW081318060426
835509LV00015B/1571